Soccer Coach Notebook

CREATED BY
21 Exercises

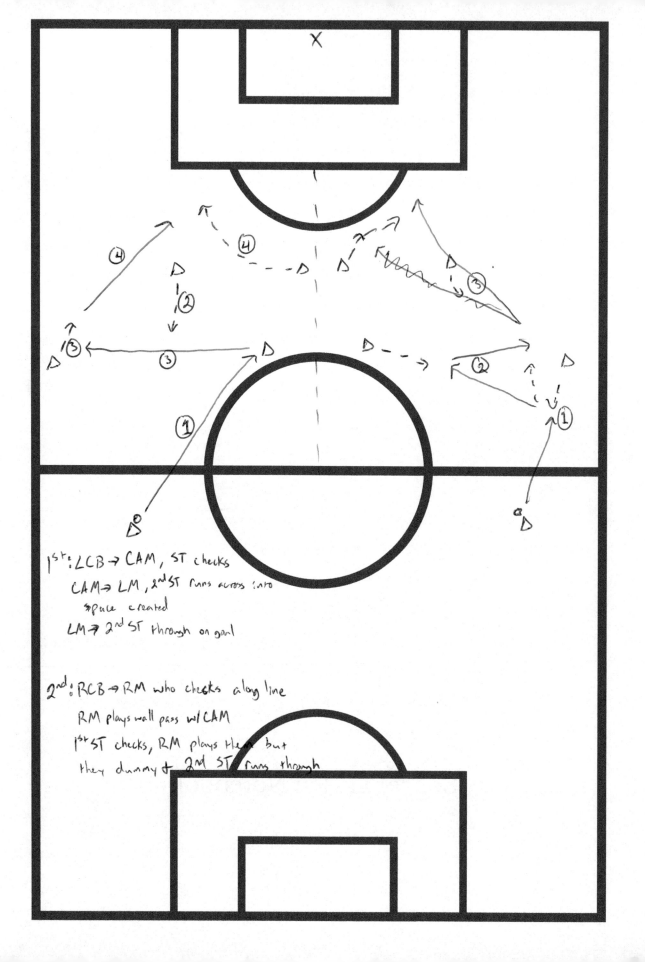

X

1st: LCB → CAM, ST checks
   CAM → LM, 2nd ST runs across into
      space created
   LM → 2nd ST through on goal

2nd: RCB → RM who checks along line
   RM plays wall pass w/ CAM
   1st ST checks, RM plays them but
   they dummy & 2nd ST runs through

13/15 girls

Date:

- Warm up
- Juggle challenges
- ~~struck~~

- Crossing/finishing reps
  ↳ wall pass/get in the box

      Brooke, Brooke

- 3 teams, team off 18 bumpers
  ↳ 2 goals, extra points for volleys/headers

- Scrimmage

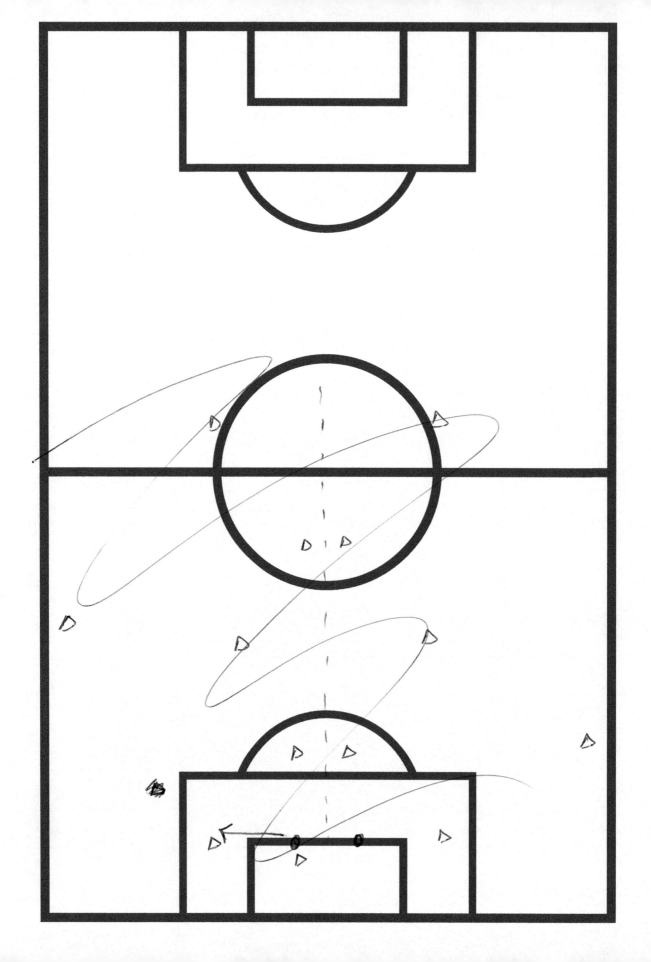

Date:

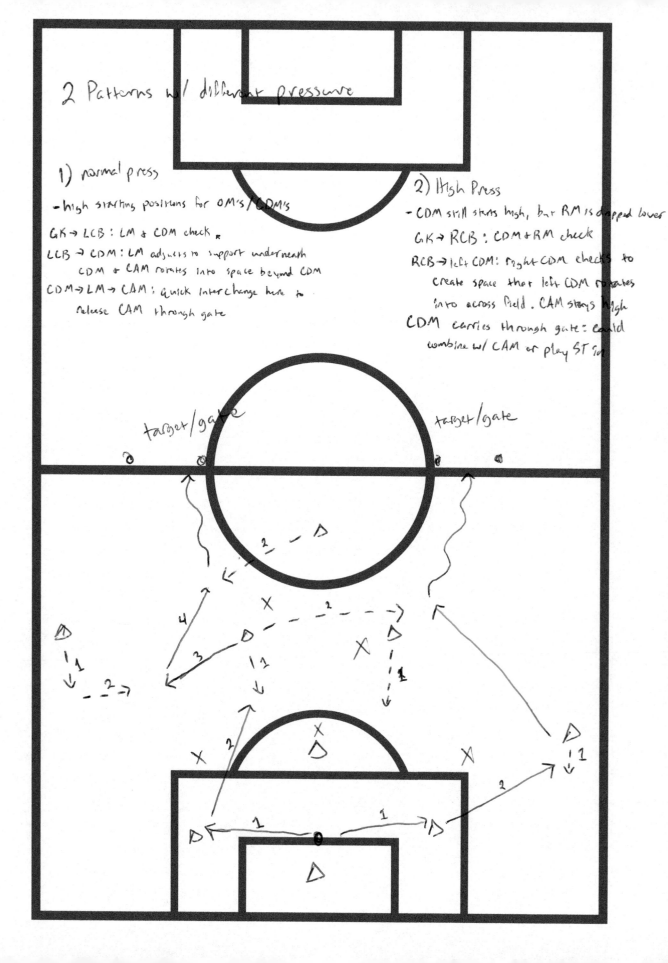

2 Patterns w/ different pressure

1) normal press

- high starting positions for OM's/CDM's

GK → LCB : LM & CDM check

LCB → CDM : LM adjusts to support underneath
    CDM & CAM rotates into space beyond CDM

CDM → LM → CAM : quick interchange here to
    release CAM through gate

2) High Press

- CDM still starts high, but RM is dropped lower

GK → RCB : CDM & RM check

RCB → left CDM : right CDM checks to
    create space that left CDM rotates
    into across field. CAM stays high

CDM carries through gate : could
combine w/ CAM or play ST in

target/gate   target/gate

Date:

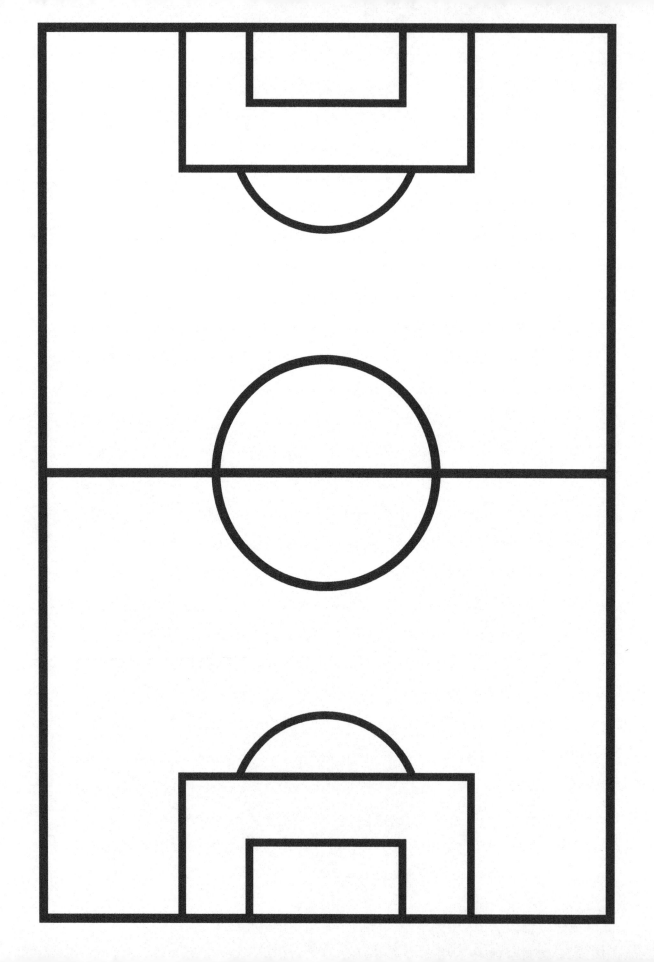

Date:

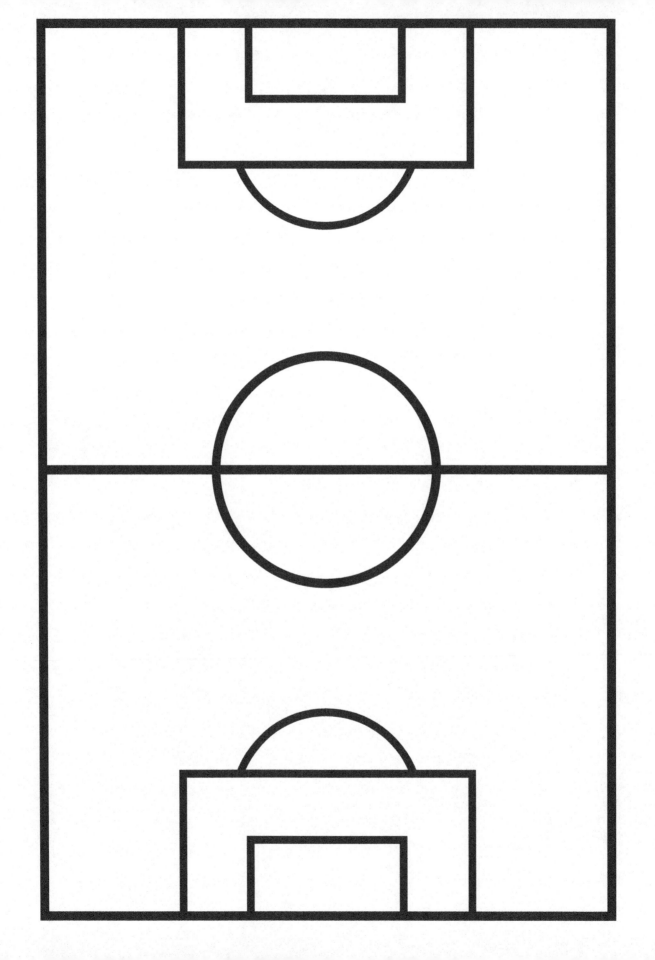

Date:

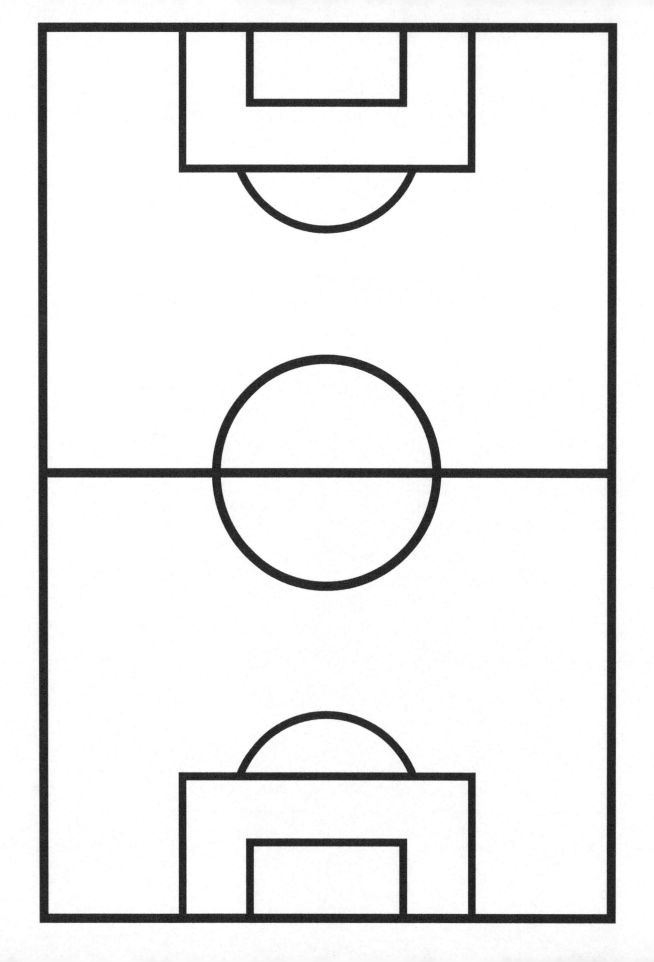

Date:

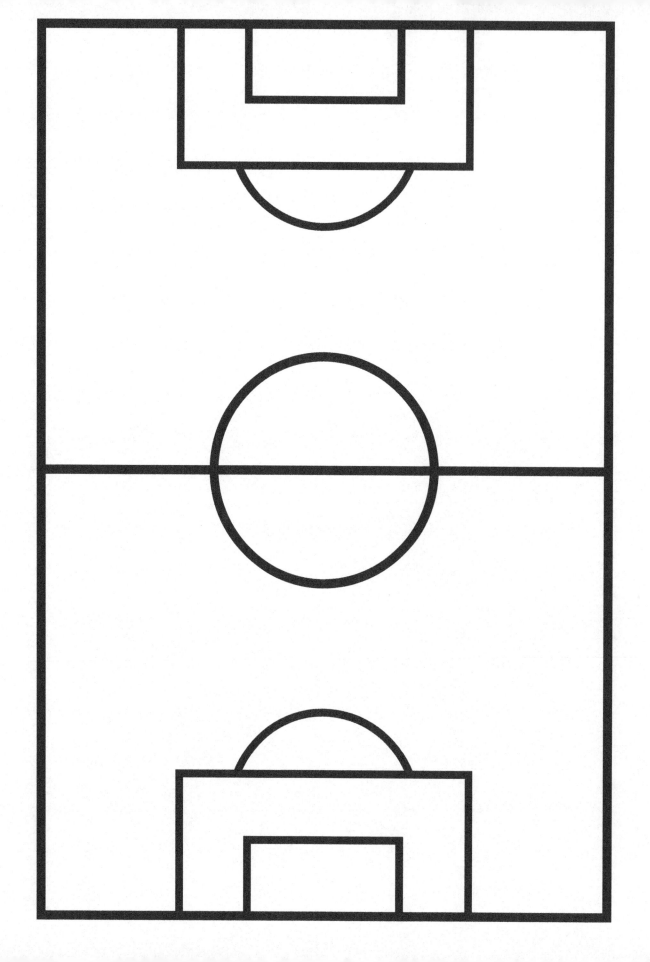

Date:

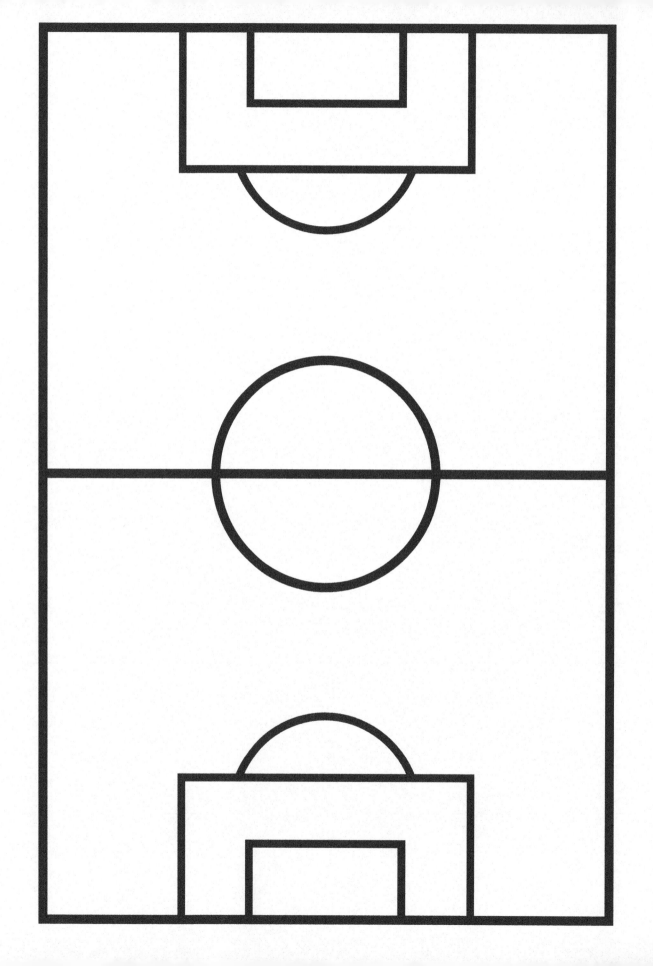

Date:

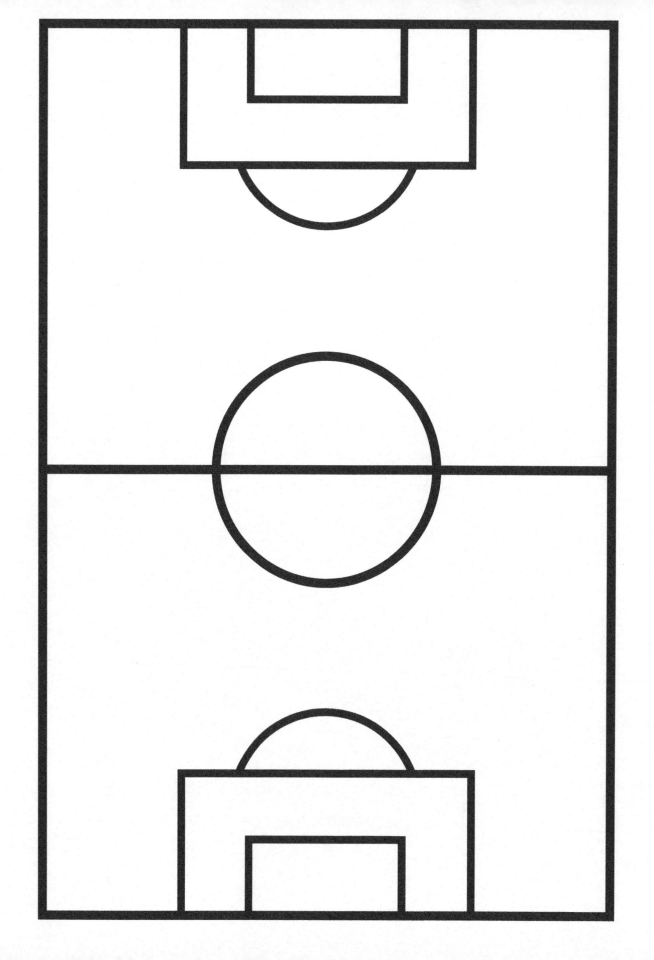

Date:

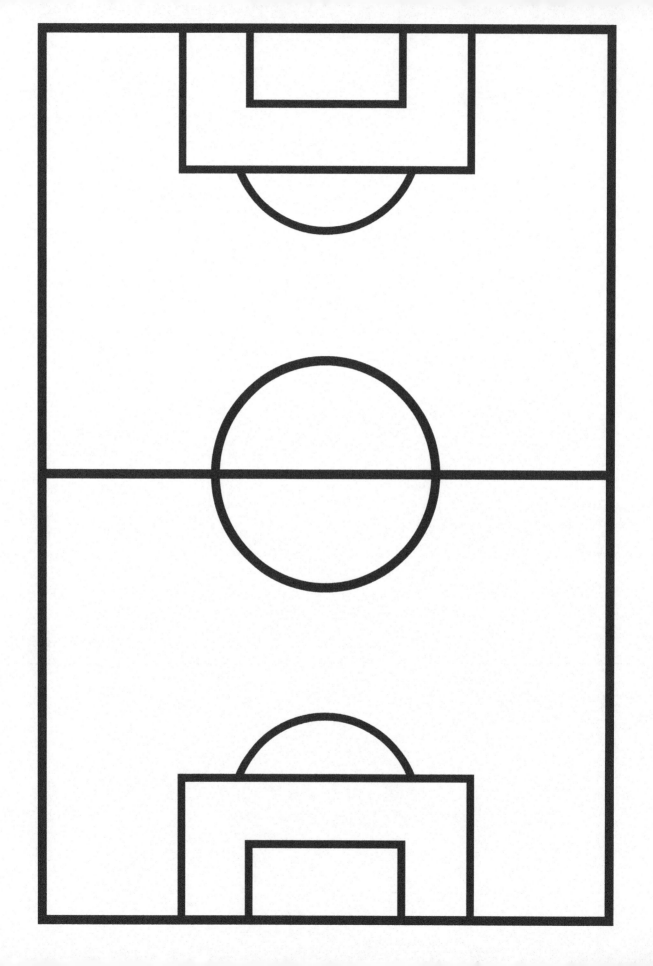

Date:

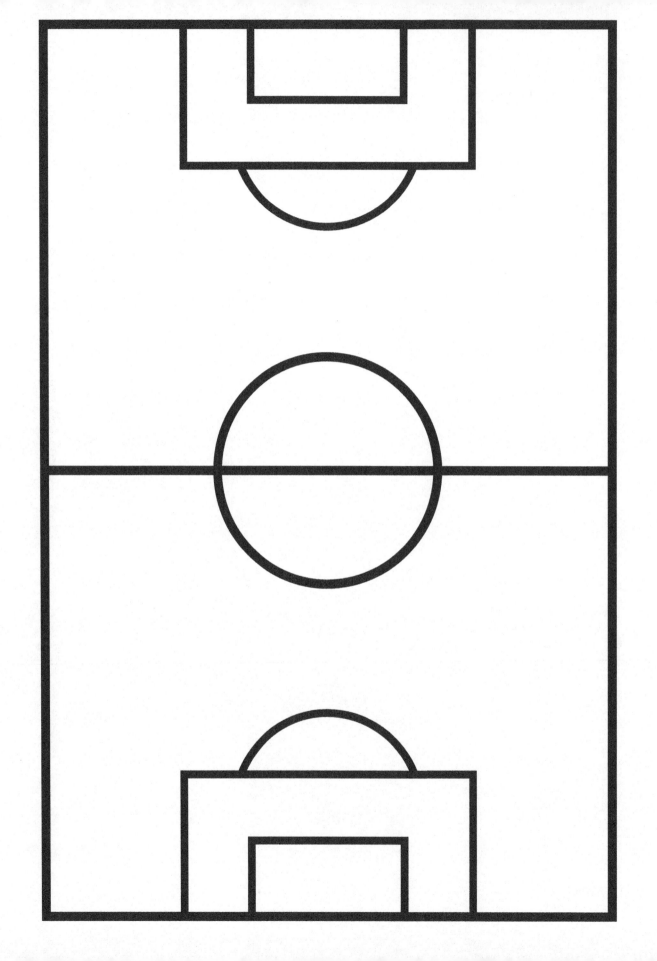

Date:

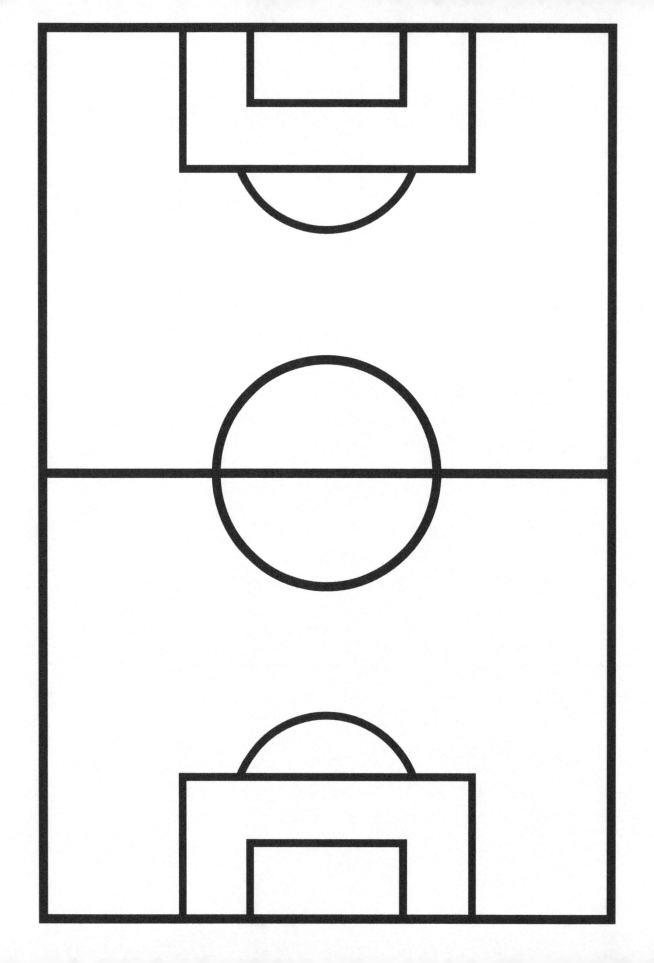

Date:

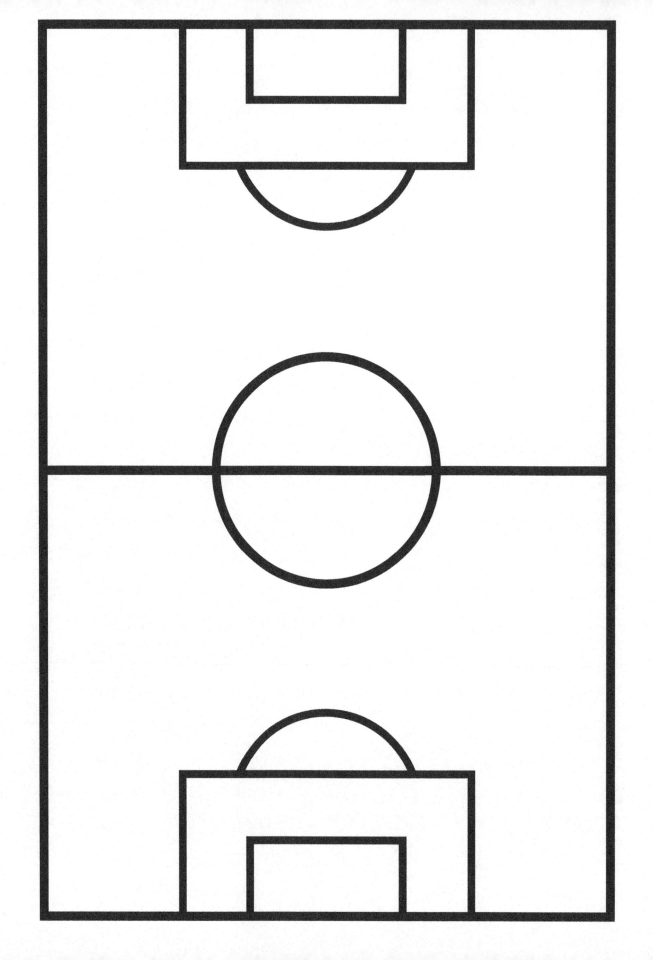

Date:

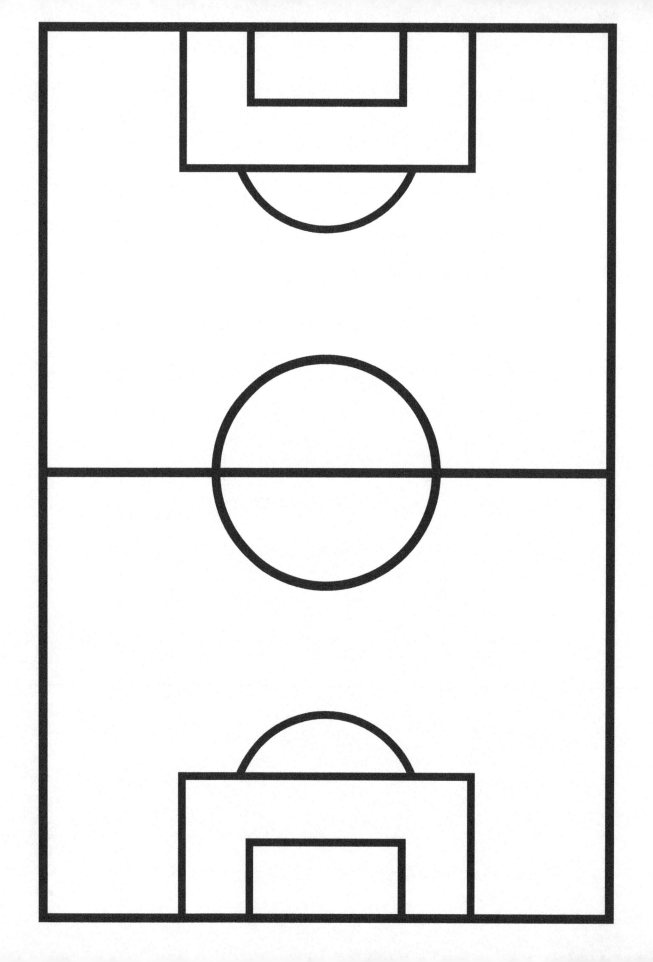

Date:

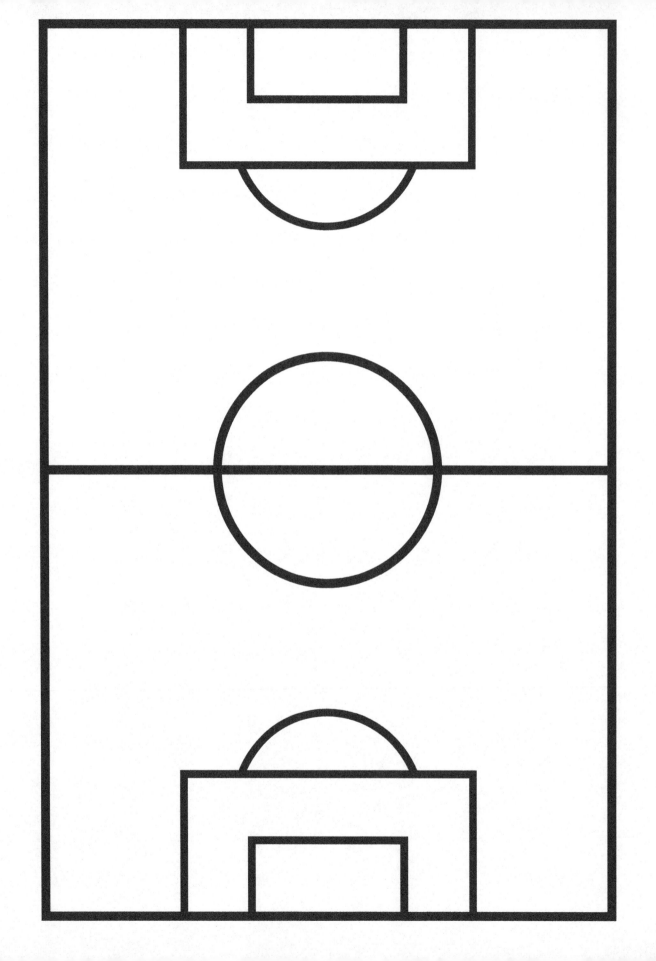

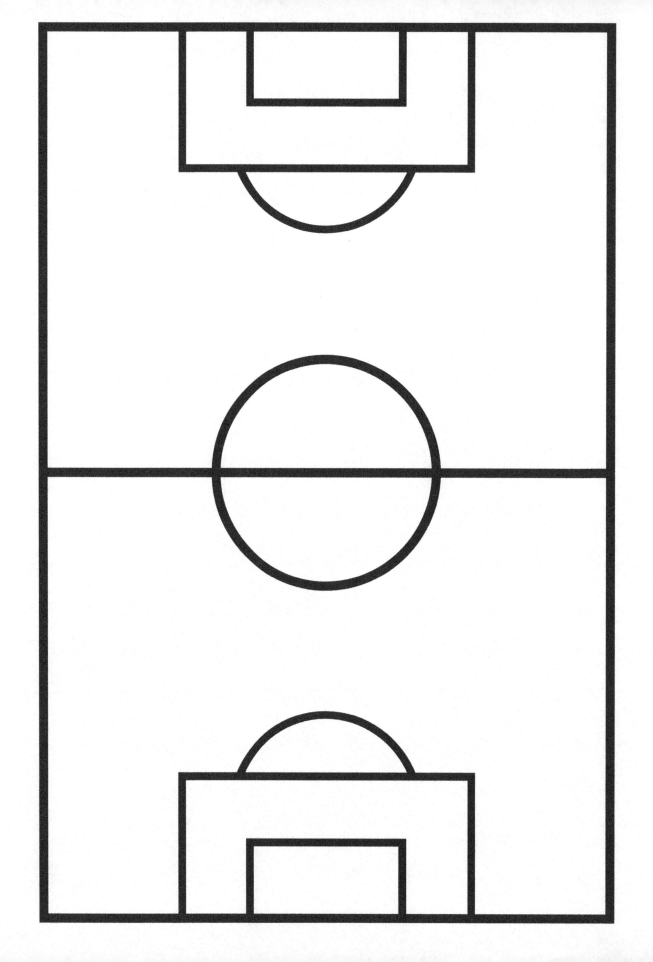

Date:

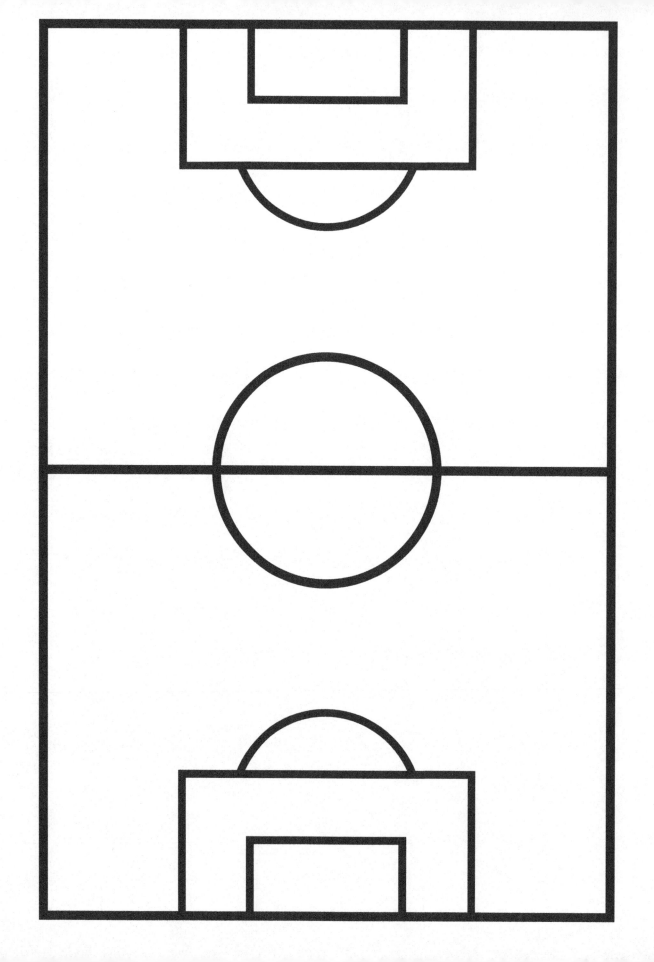

Date:

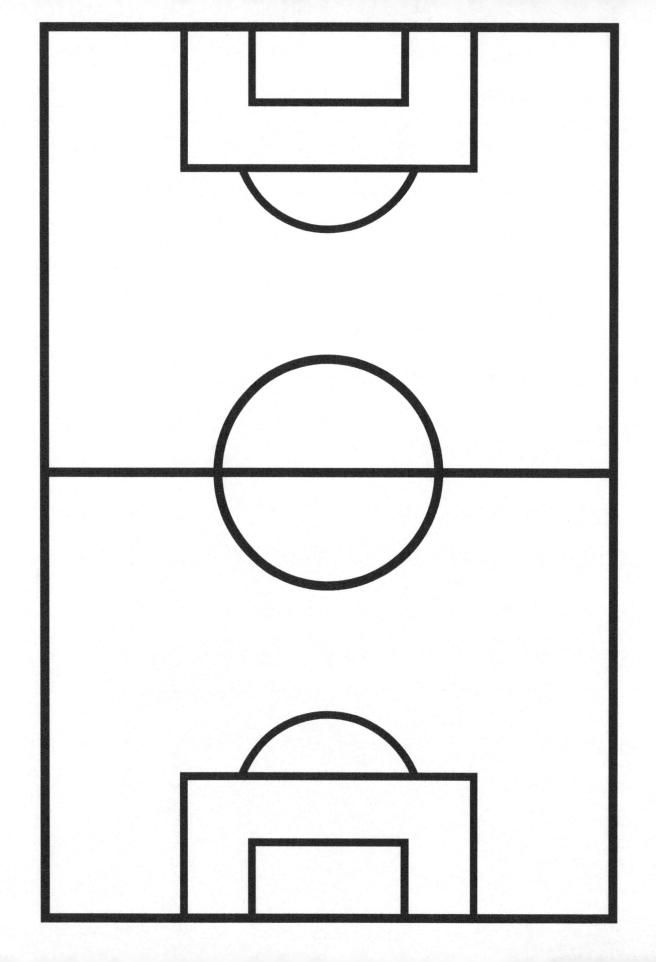

Date:

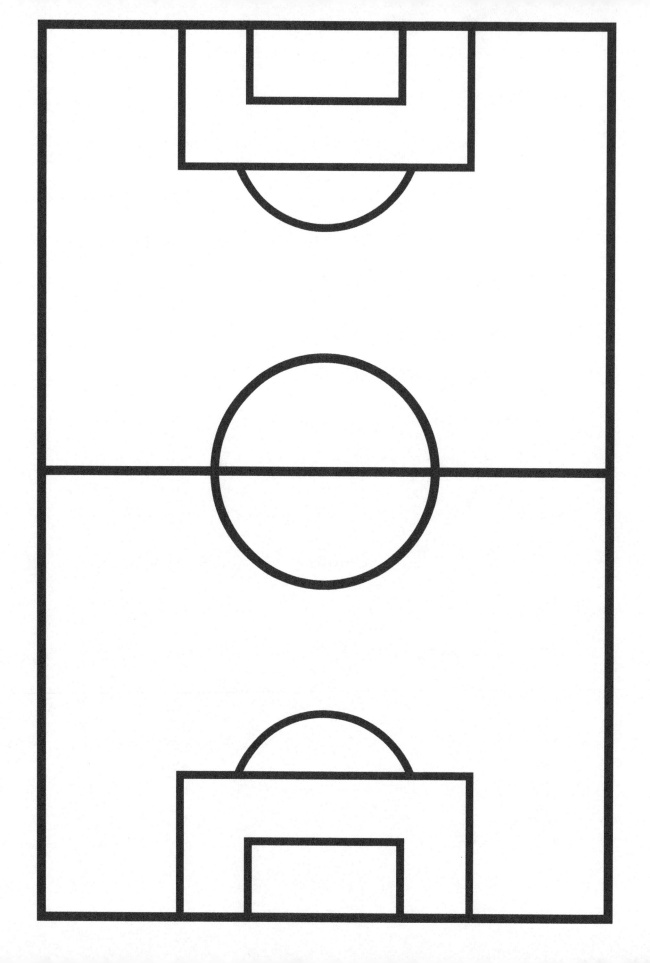

Date:

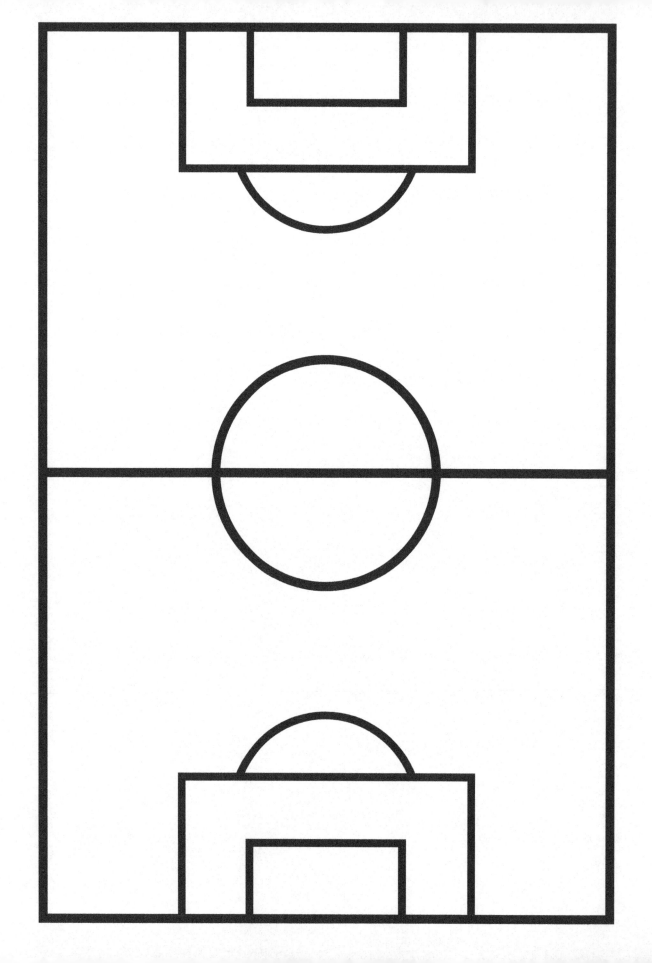

Date:

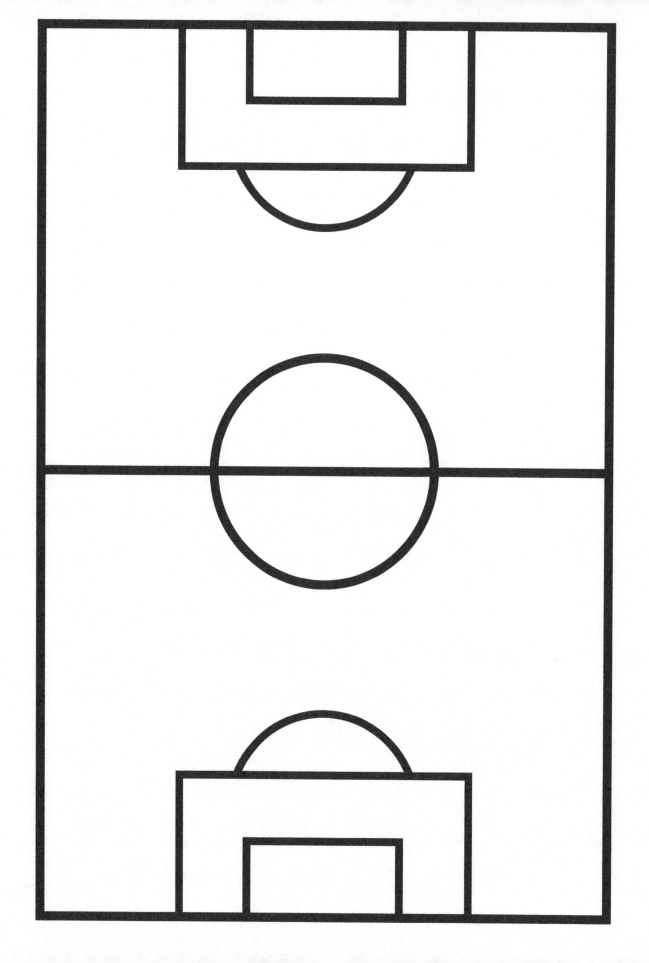

Date:

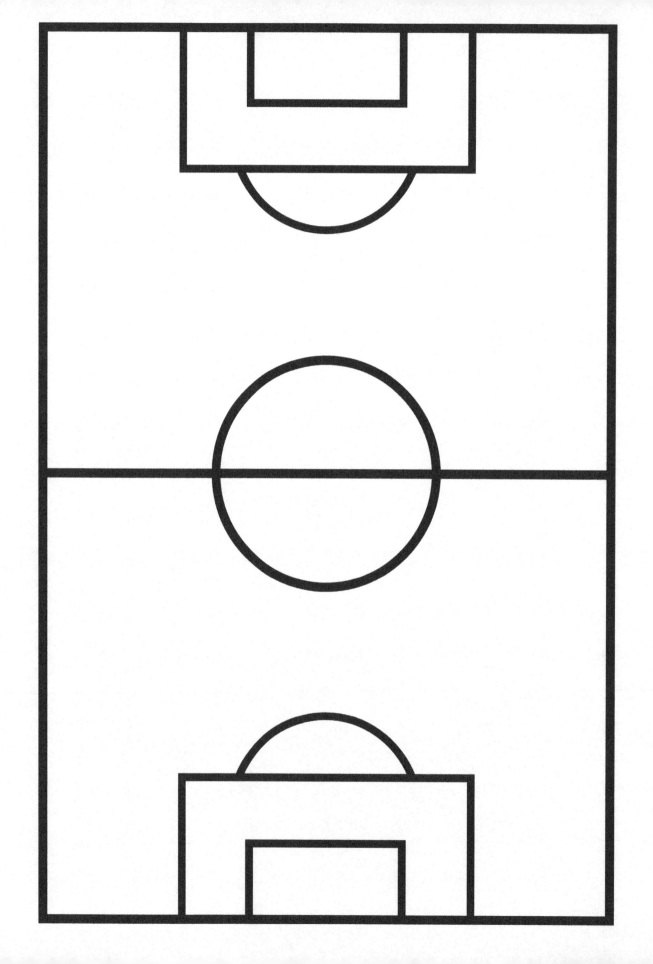

Date:

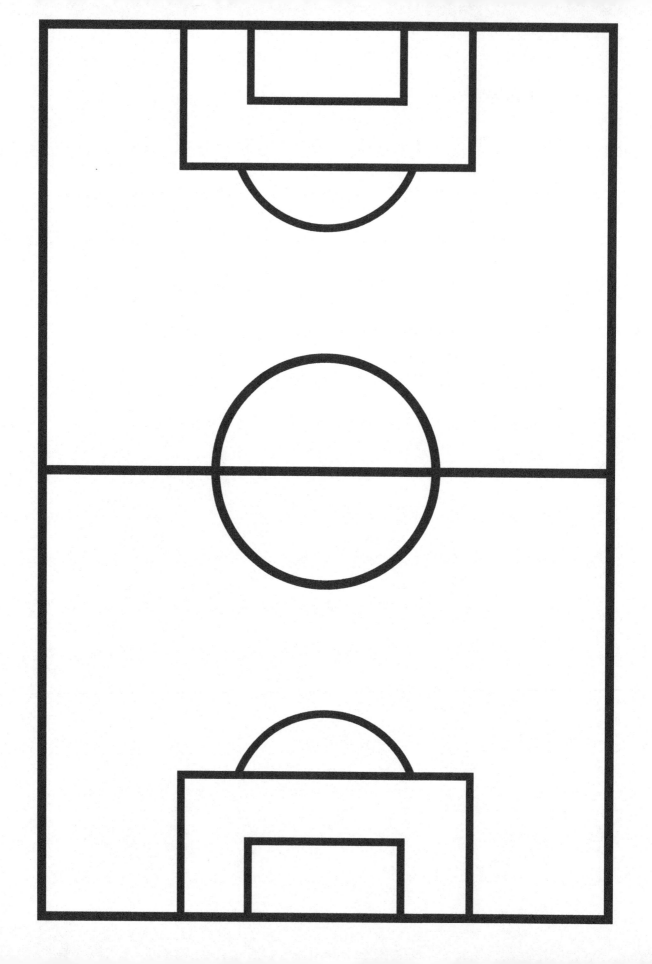

Date:

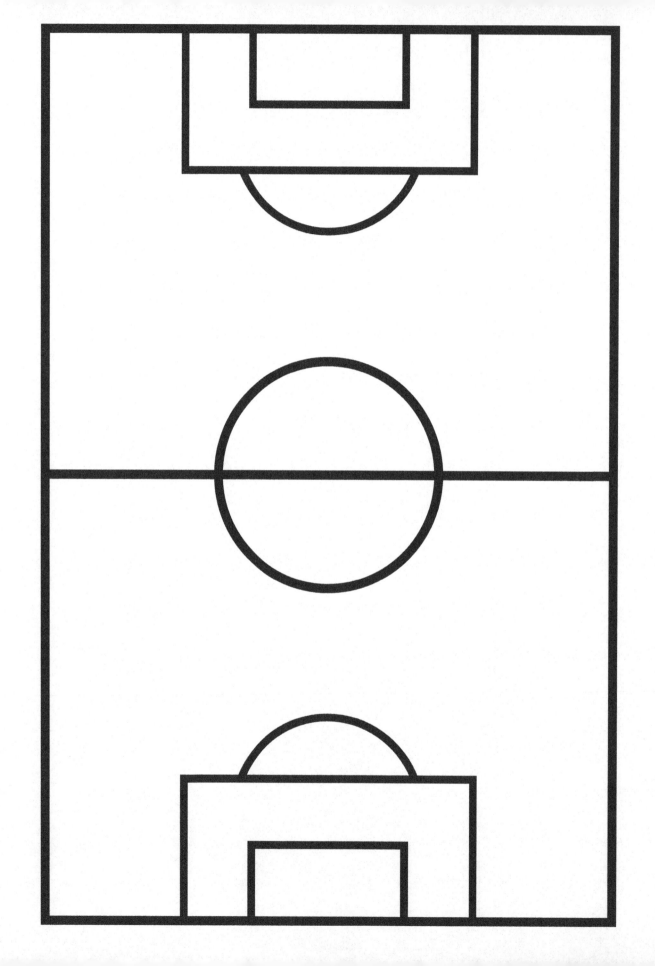

Date:

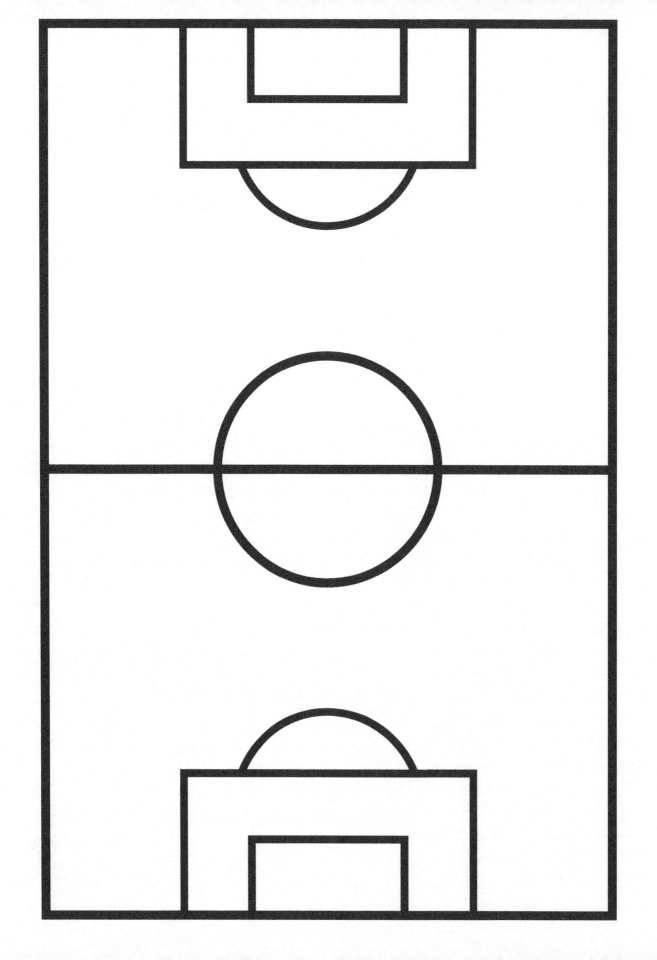

Date:

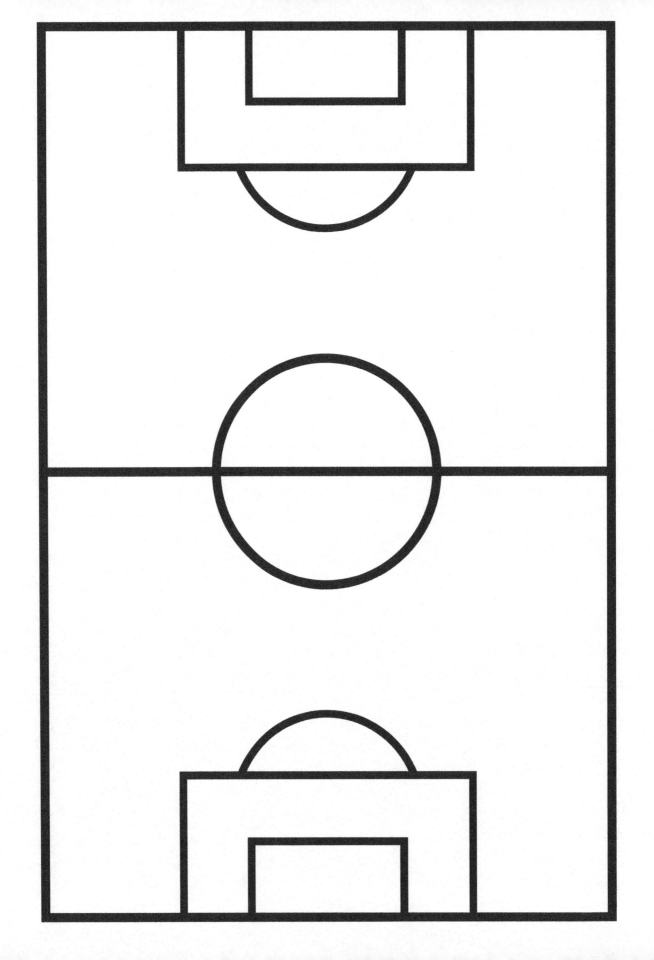

Date:

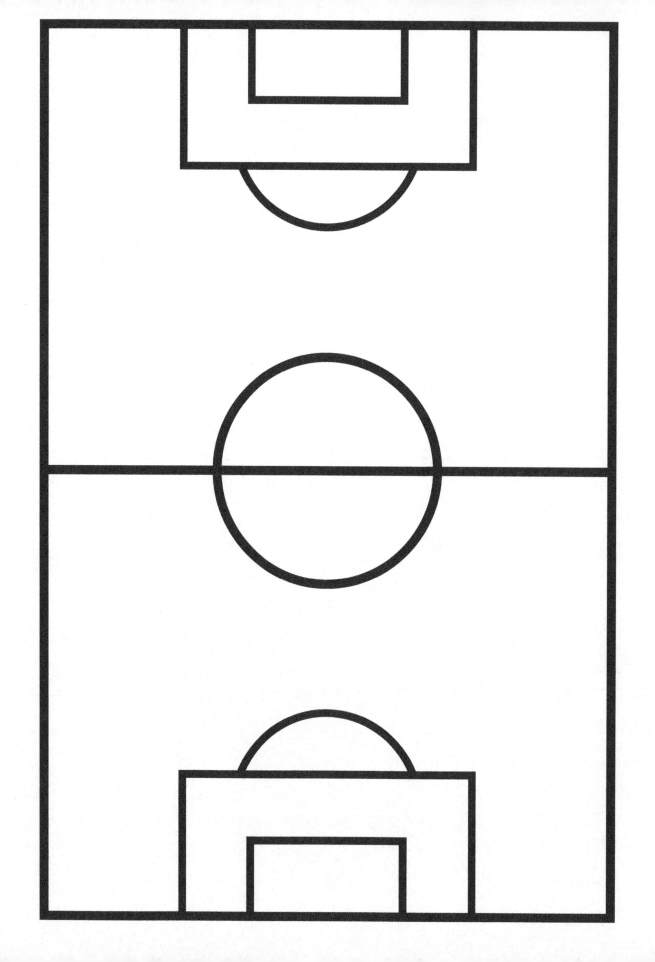

Date:

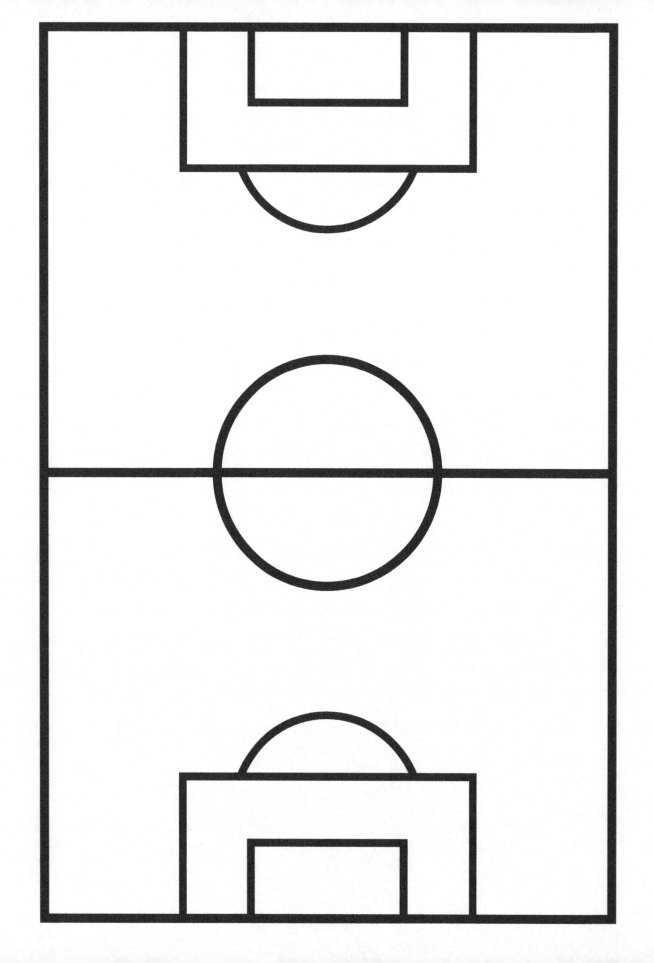

Date:

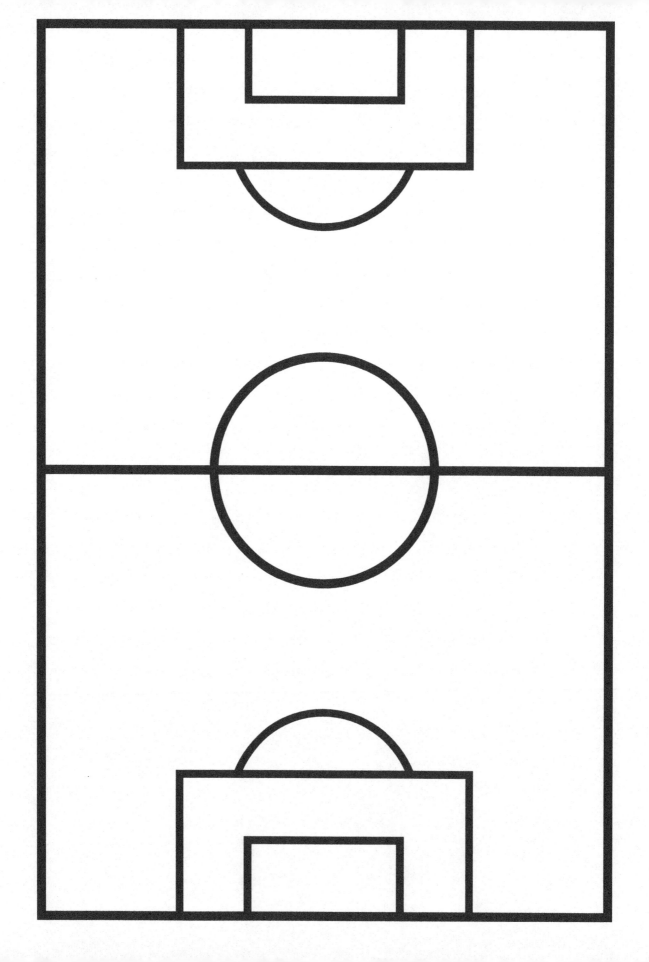

Date:

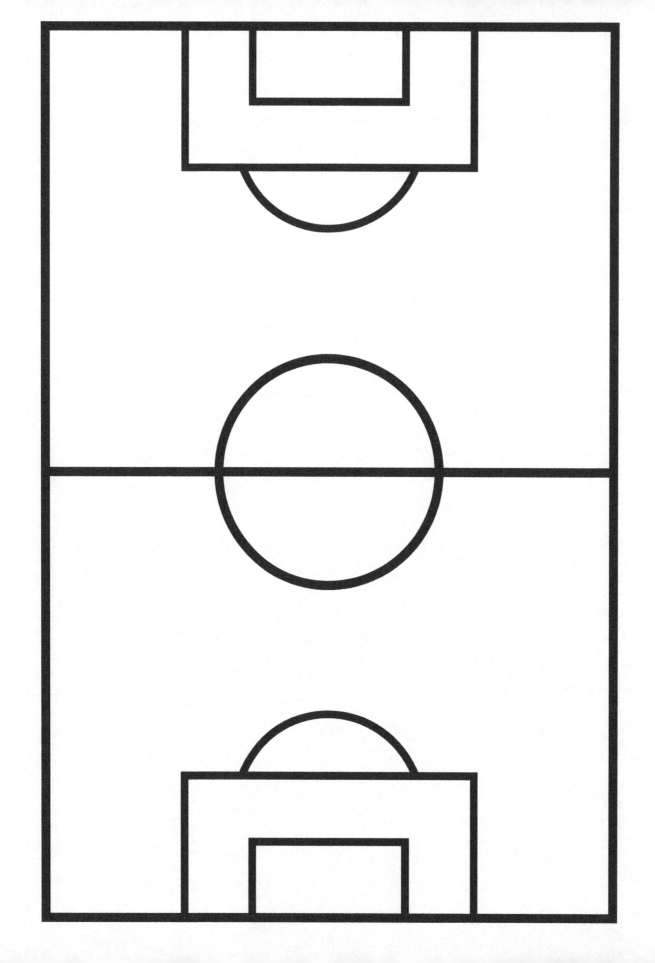

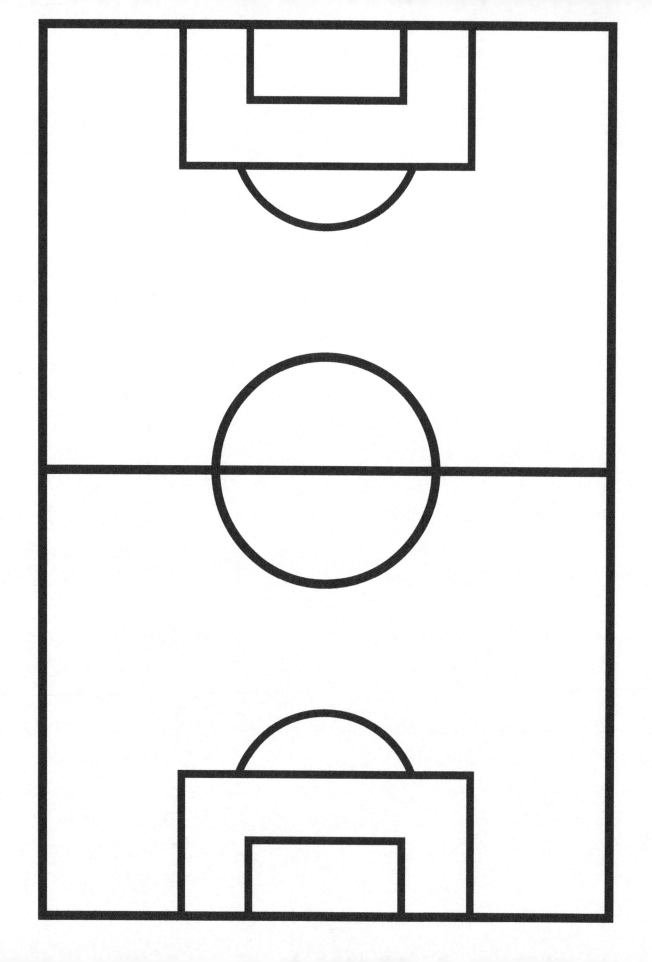

Date:

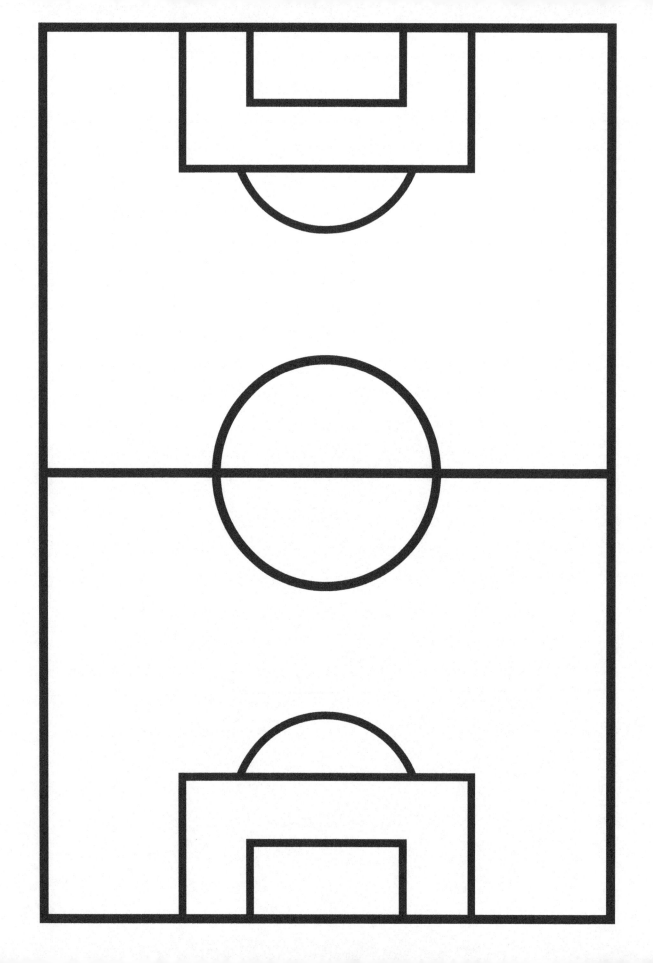

Date:

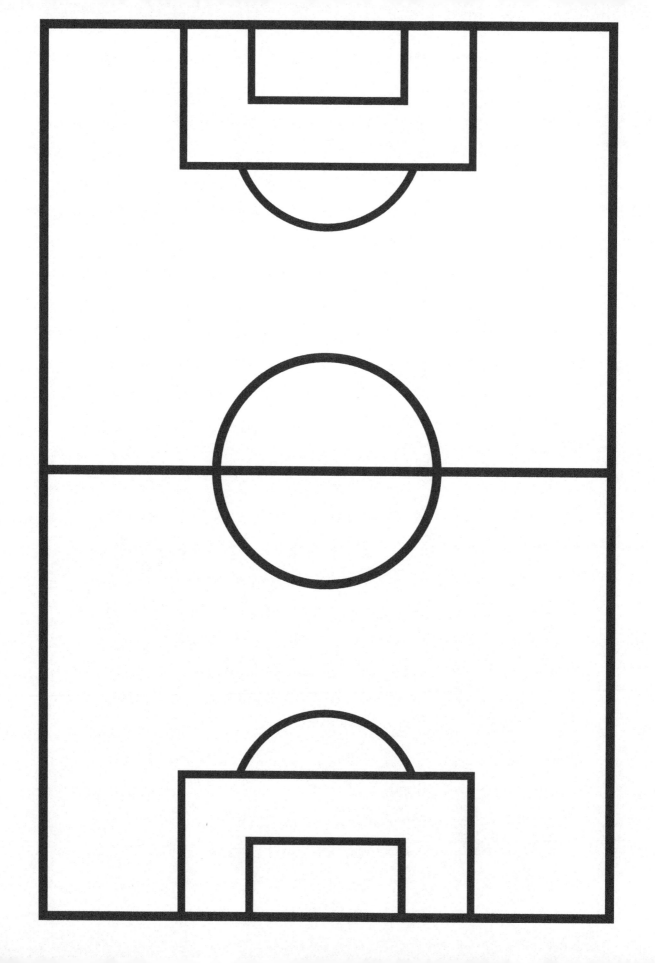

Date:

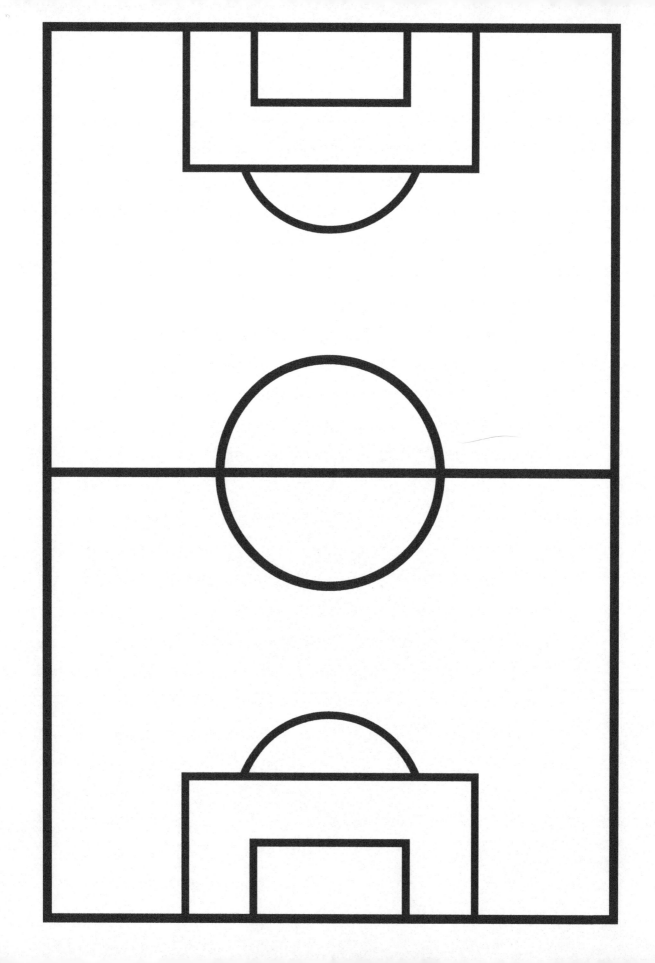

Date:

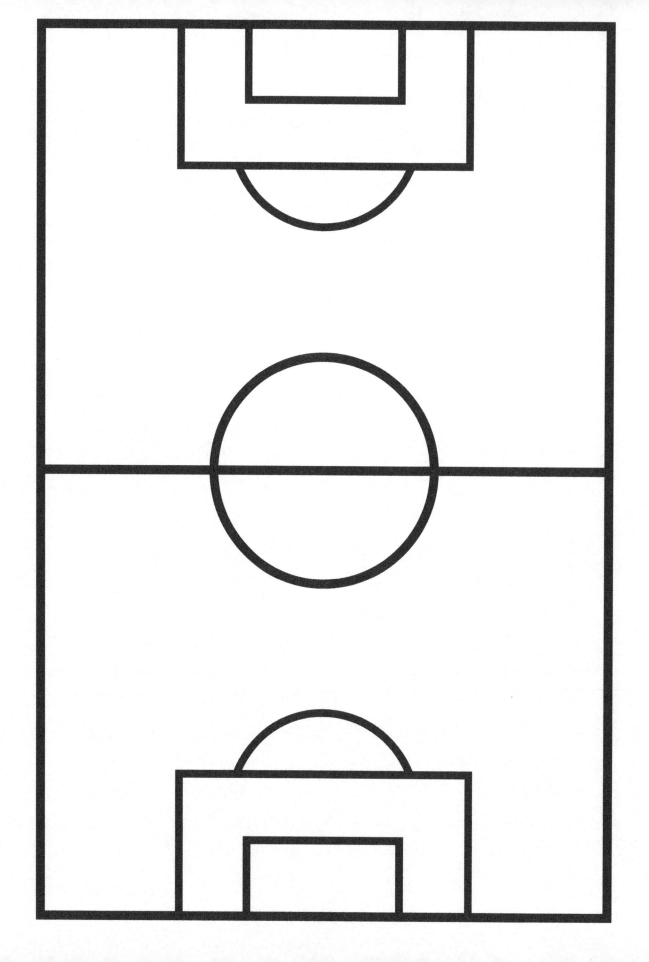

Date:

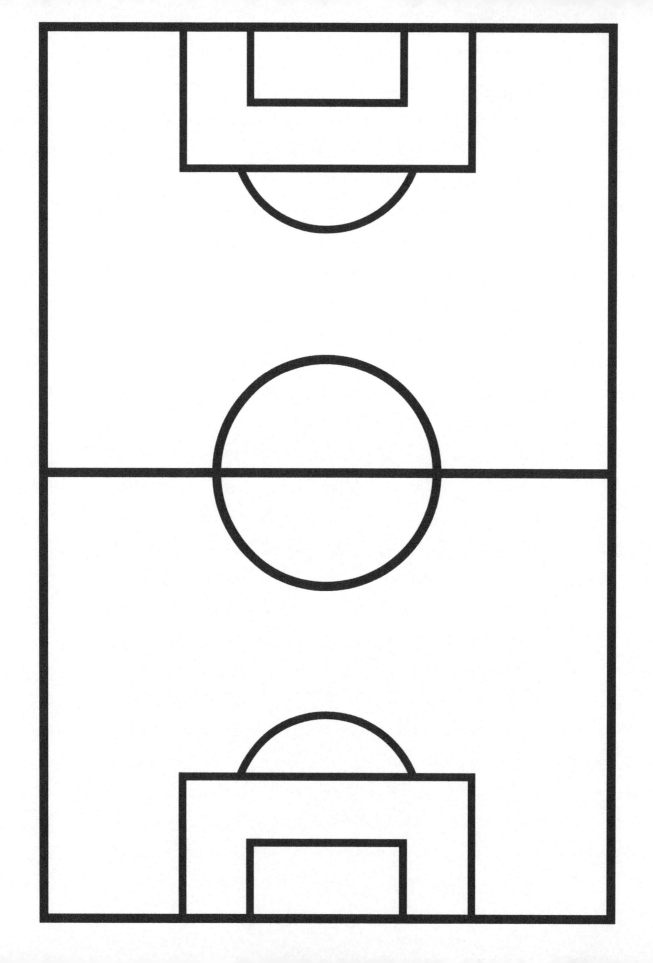

Date:

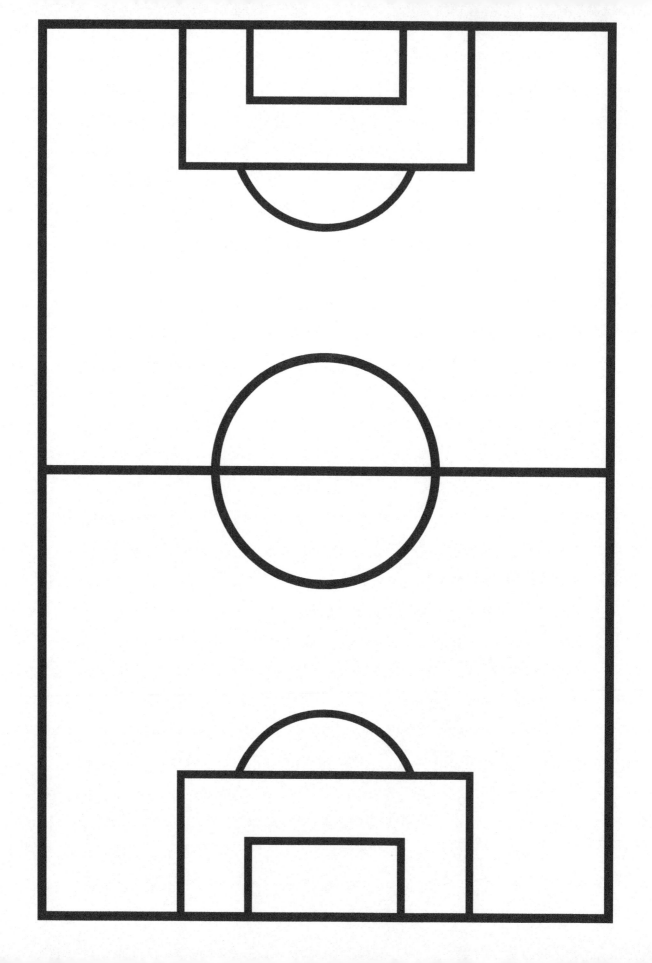

Date:

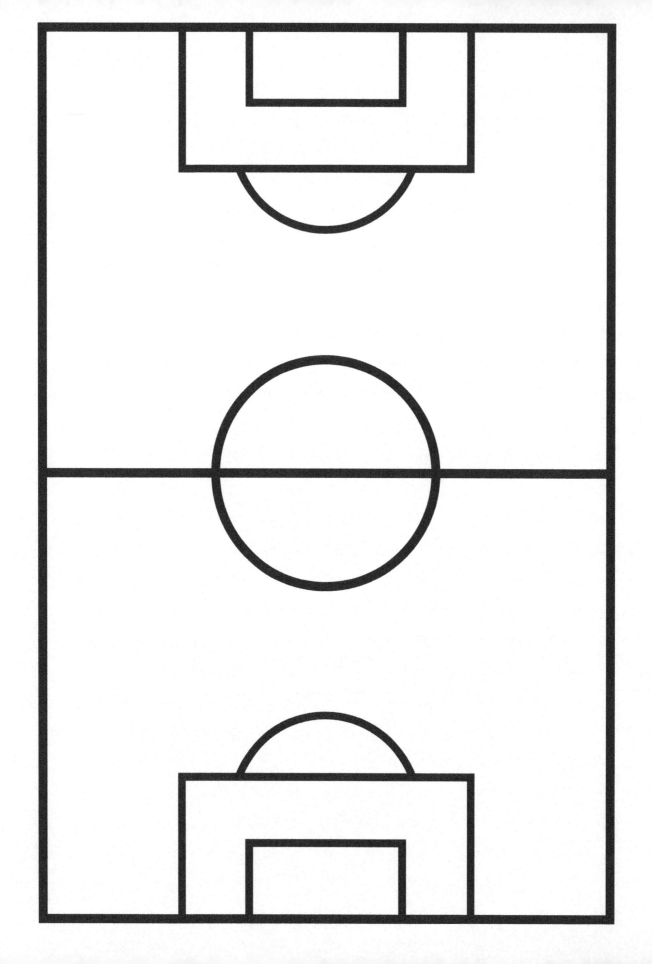

Date:

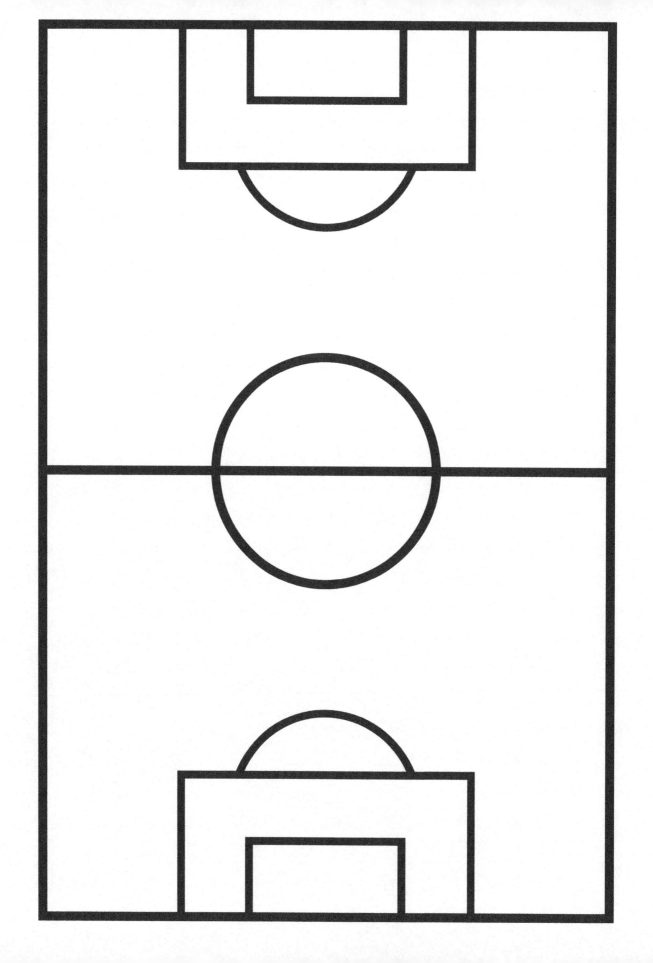

Date:

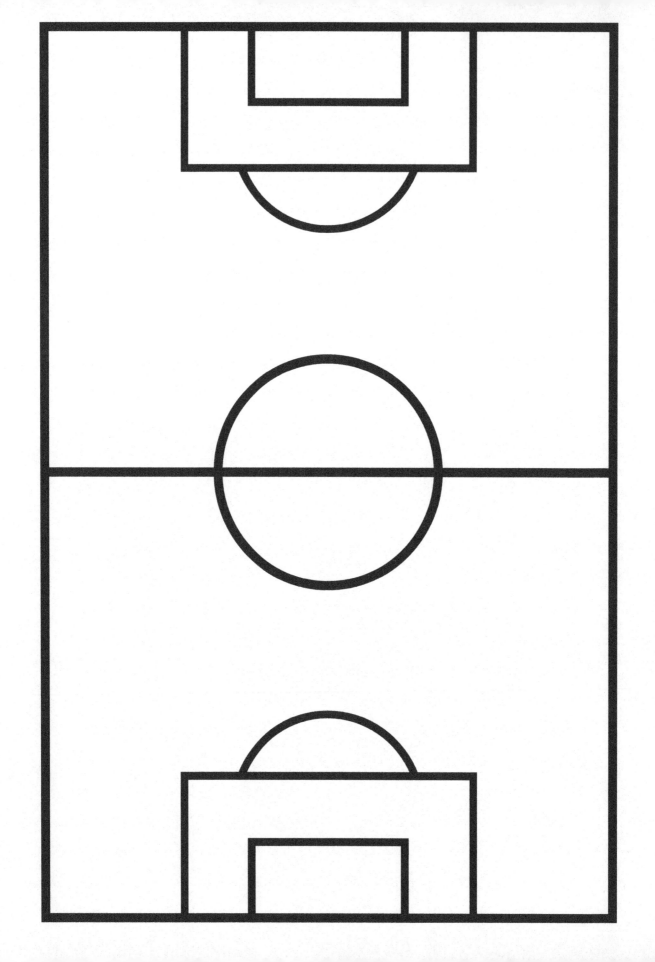

Date:

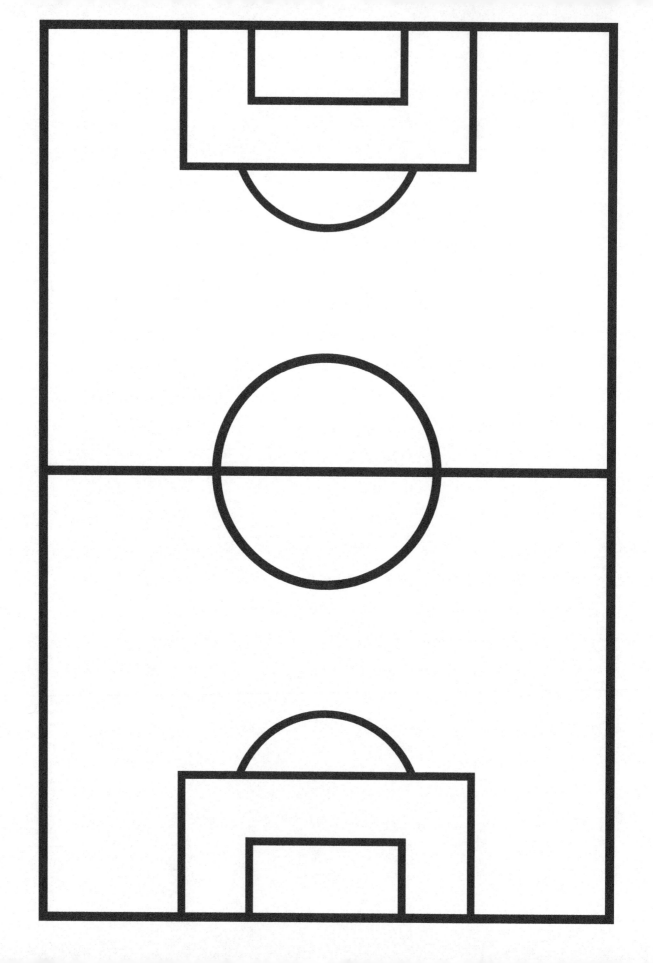

Date:

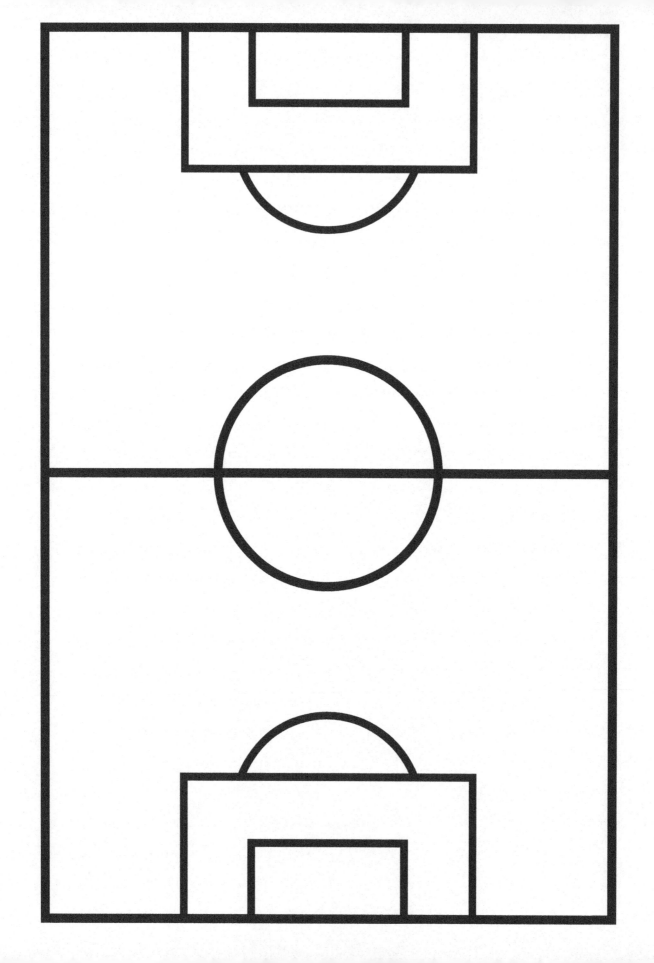

Date:

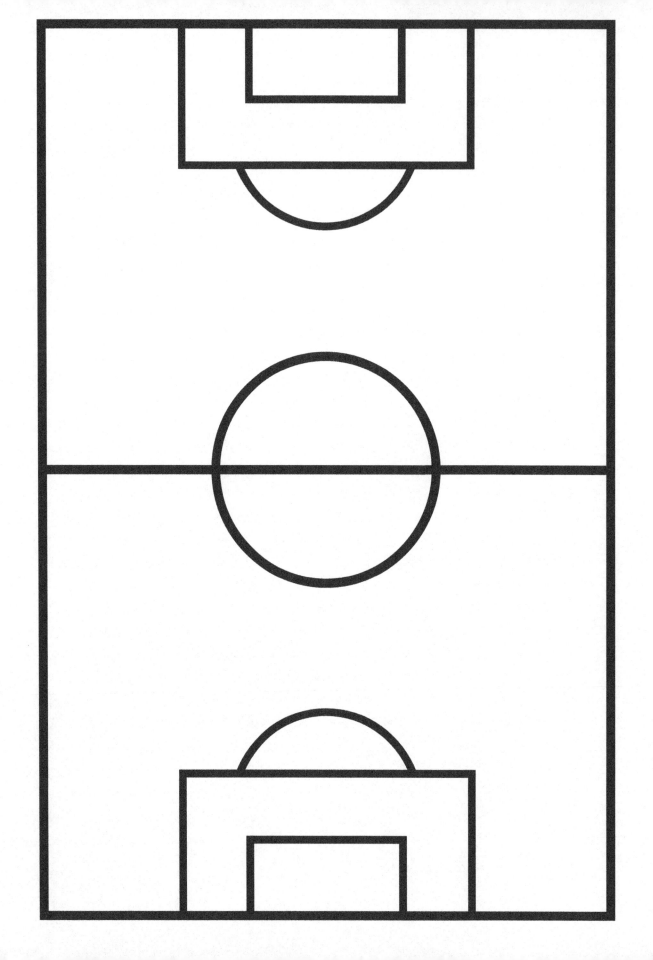

Date:

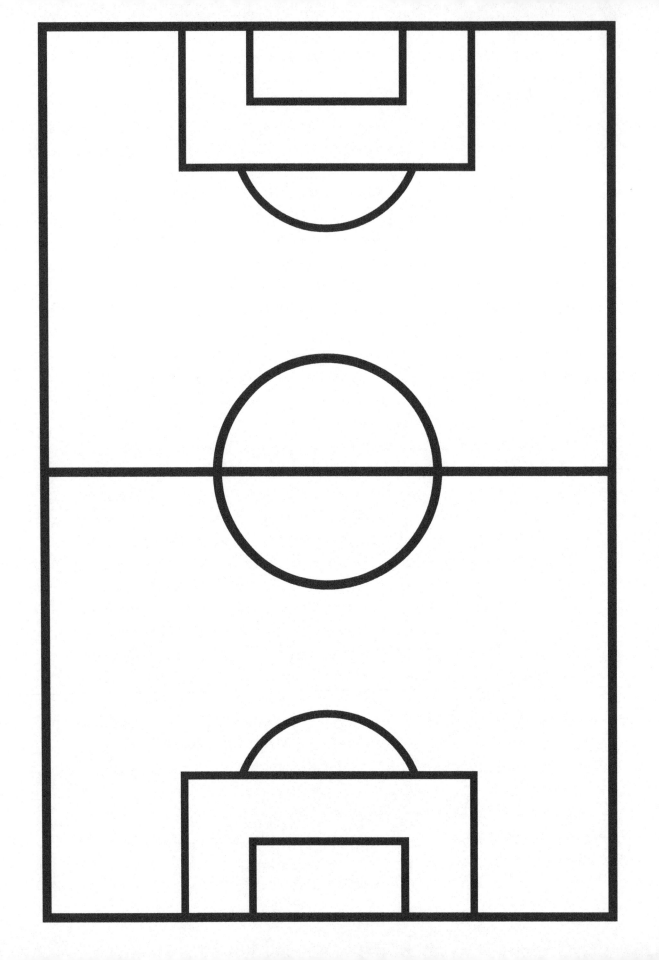

Date:

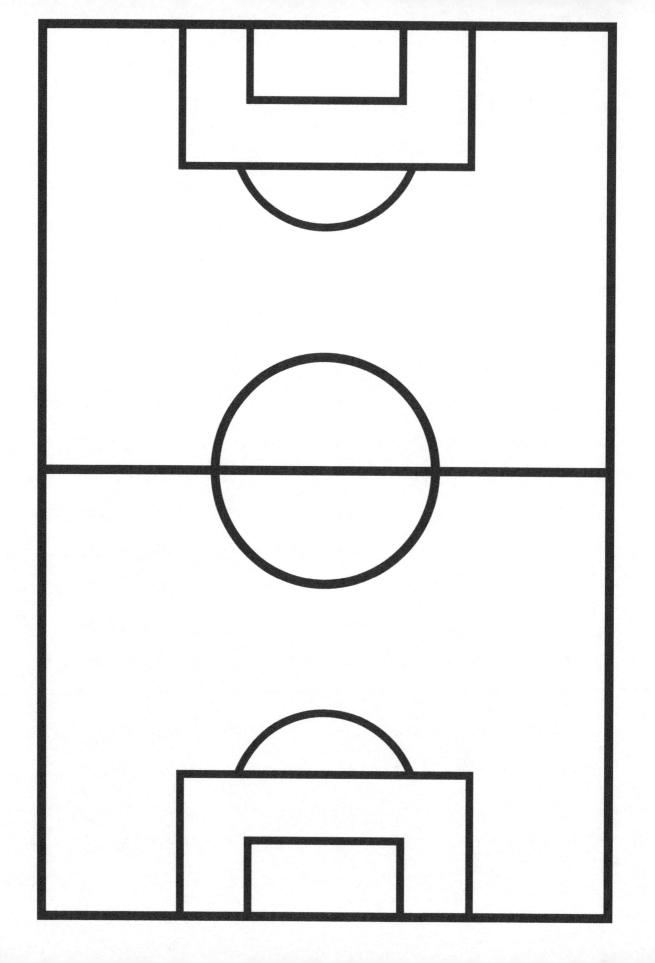

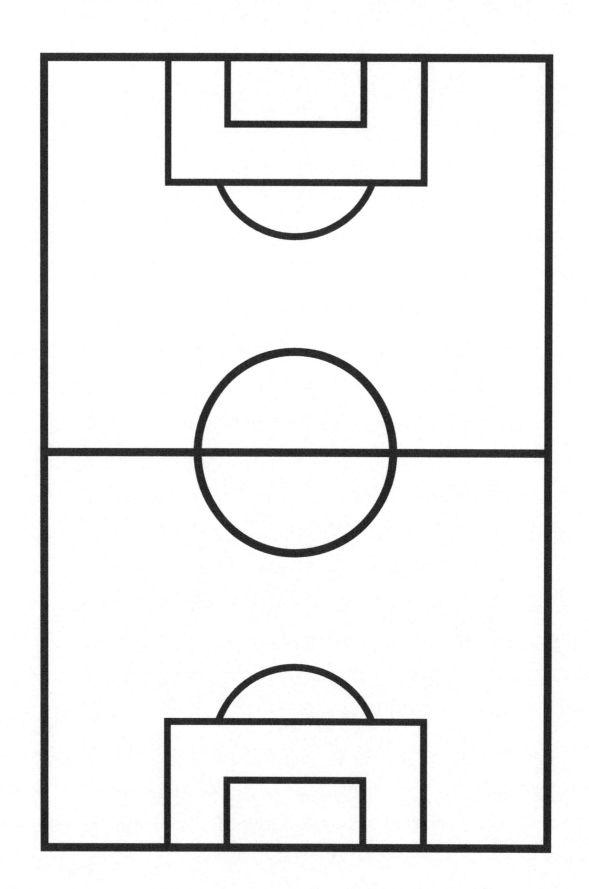

Date:

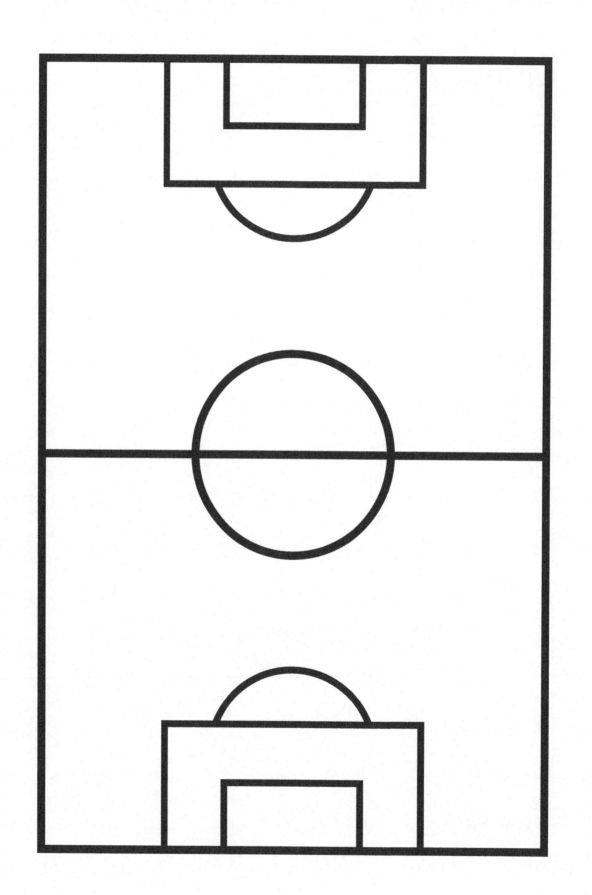

Date:

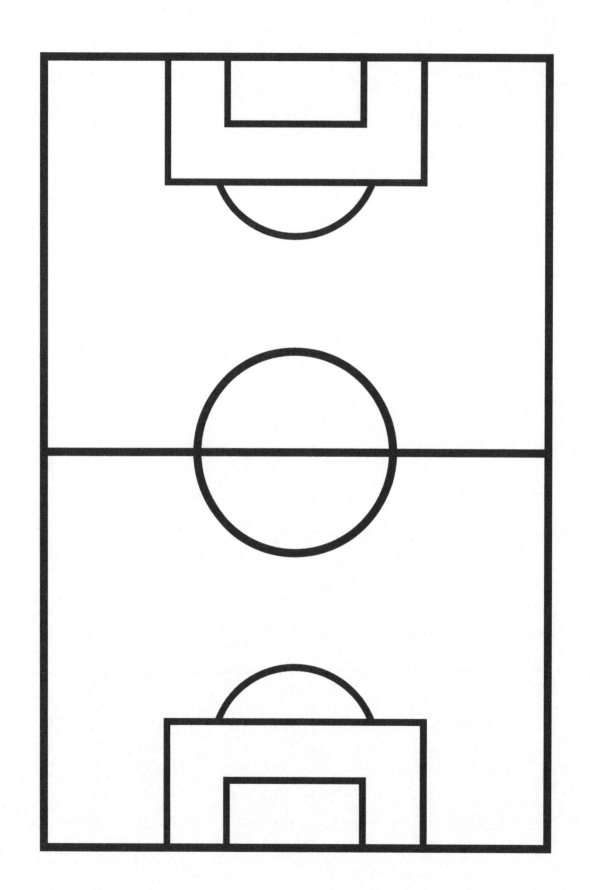

Date:

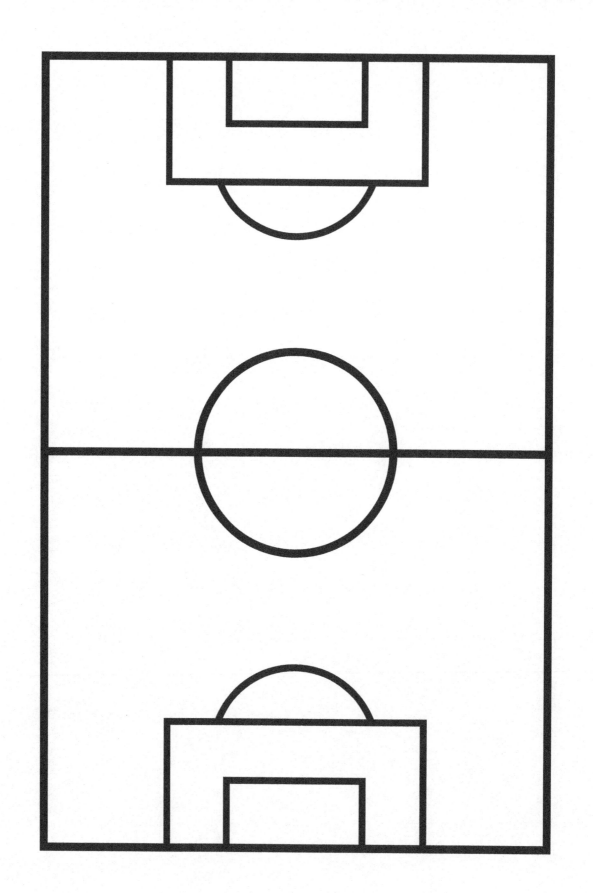

Date:

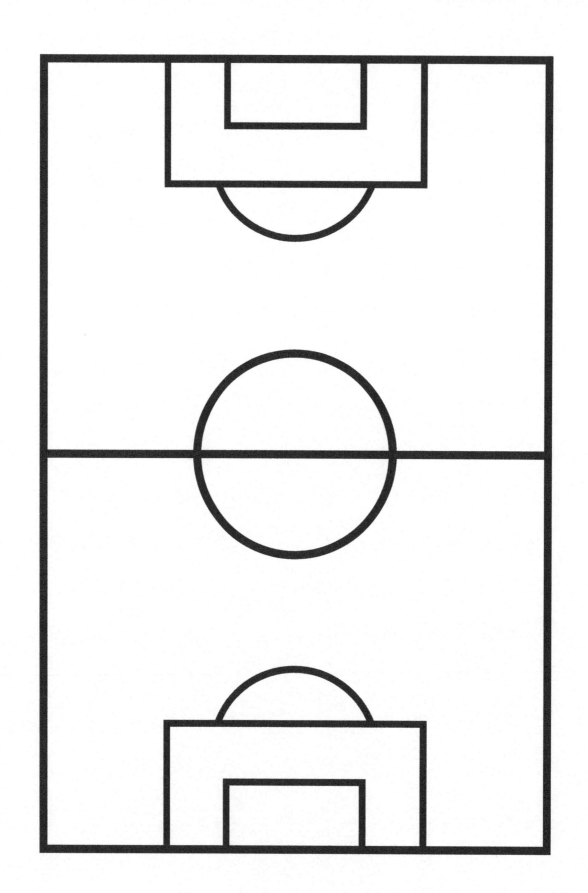

Date:

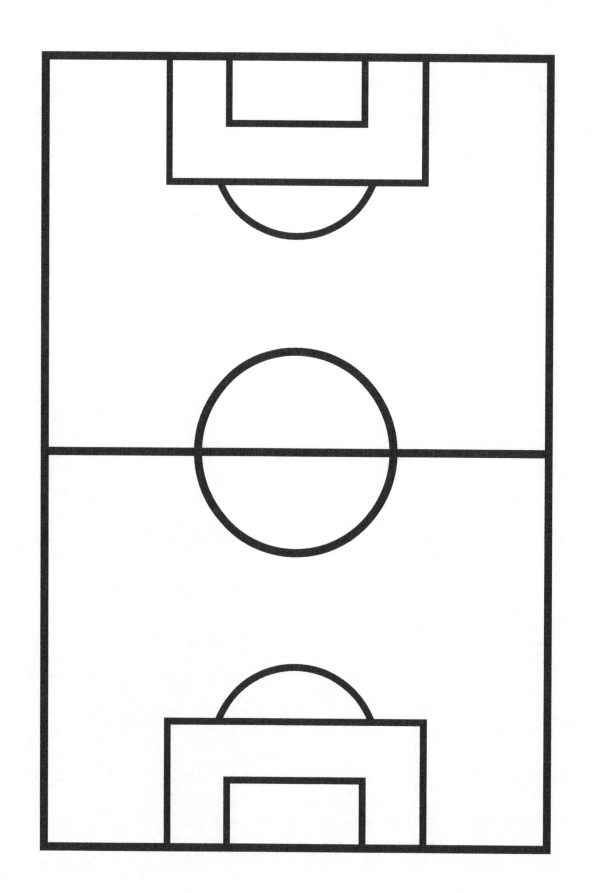

Date:

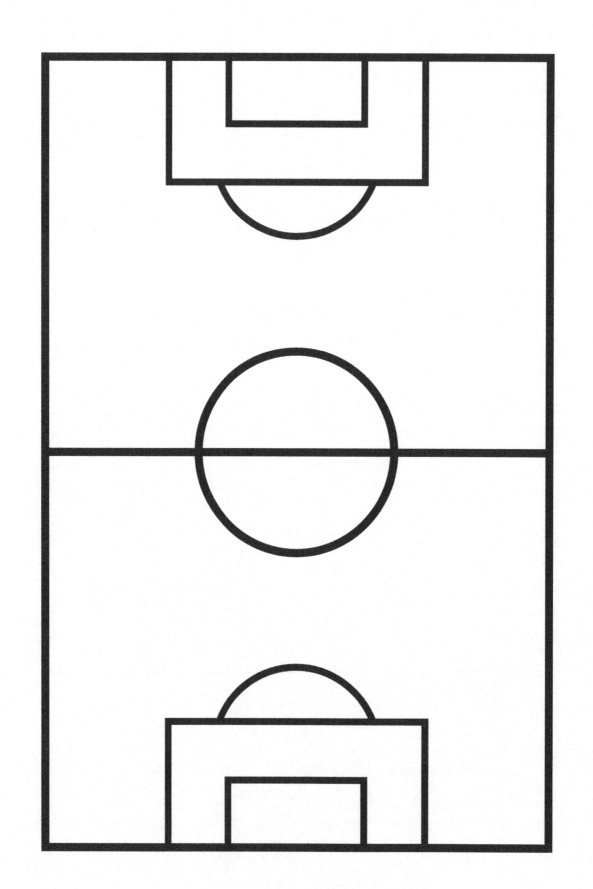

Date:

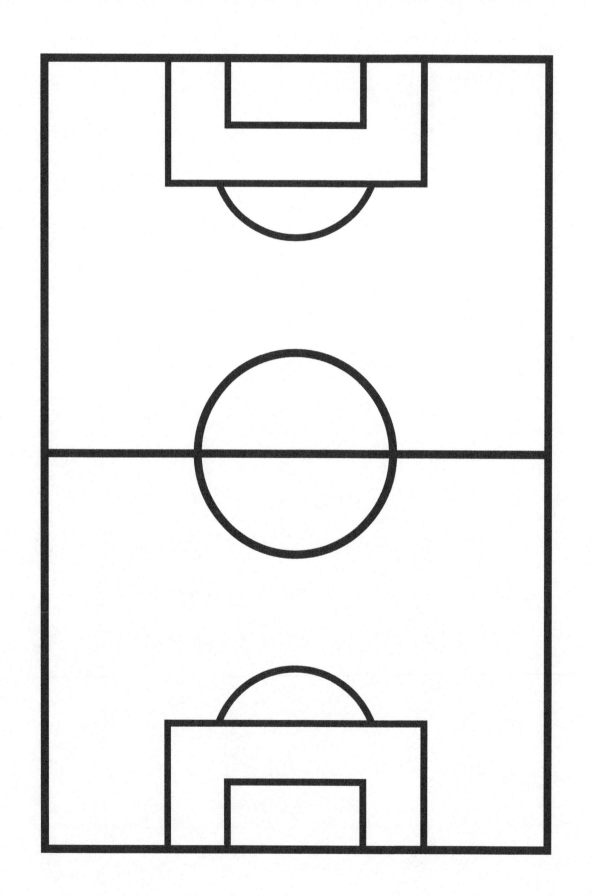

Date:

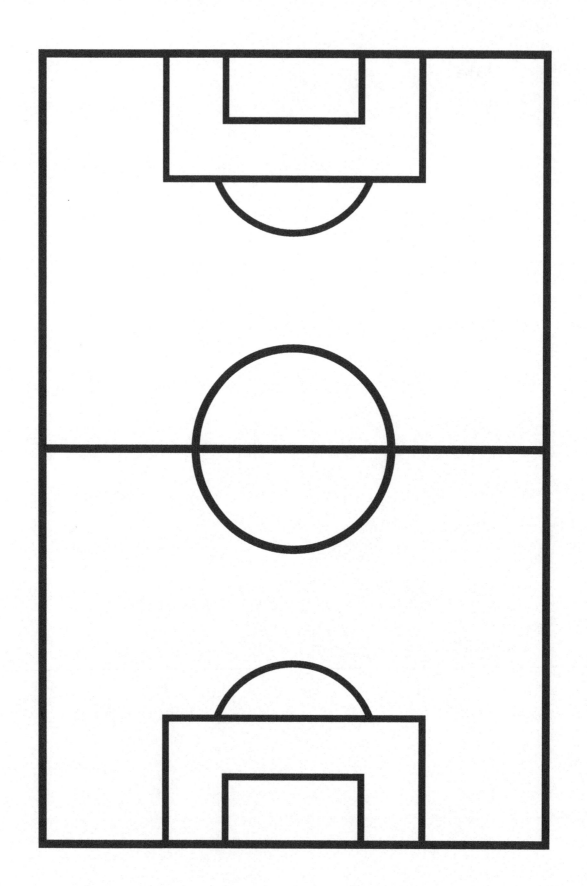

Date:

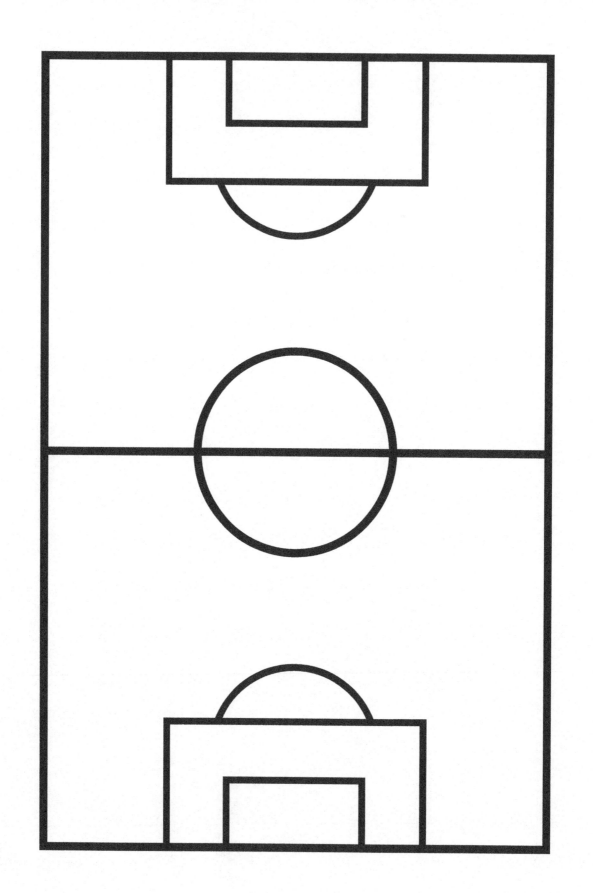

Date:

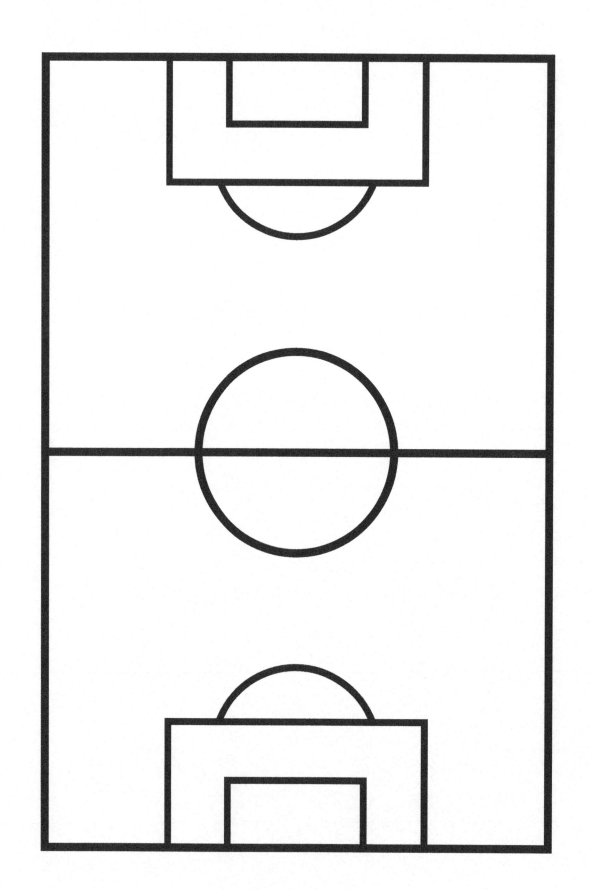

Date:

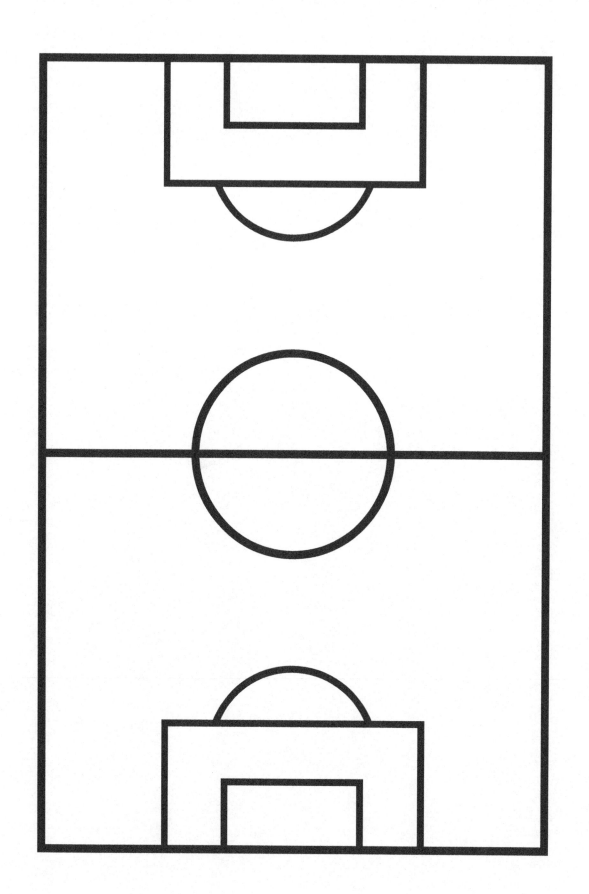

Date:

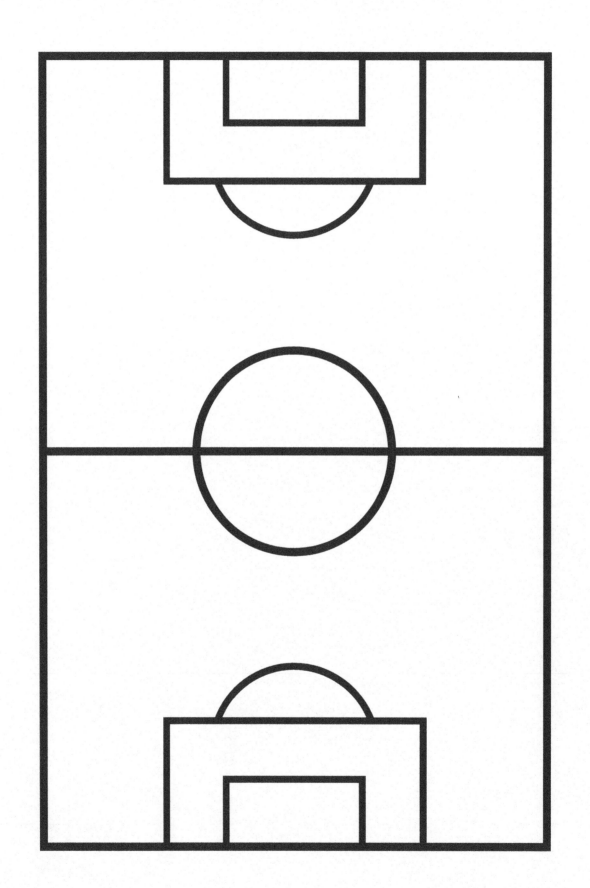

Date:

Soccer Coach Notebook

CREATED BY

21 Exercises

Made in the USA
Monee, IL
12 December 2019

18458108R00066